BREATHE, FOCUS, ATTACK

A Triple-Threat System for Creating the Life You Want

IAN SCHECHTER

"*I was waiting for something extraordinary to happen,*
but as the years wore on nothing ever did unless I caused it."

CHARLES BUKOWSKI

This book is dedicated to my mother,
who constantly reminds me how she didn't drop me
on my head as a child.

Acknowledgments

Special thanks to the rest of my family: Dad, Noah and Matthew. You have all taught me so much, and I love you.

Contents

BREATHE, FOCUS, ATTACK

A Triple-Threat System for Creating the Life You Want

Chapter One:

It's Never Too Late

IN THIS FIRST CHAPTER, we're going to discuss why it's never too late to make your life better, but we're also going to dig into a way of thinking about how we approach challenges in life. I call this *Breathe, Focus, Attack*. As you may have guessed, it has three steps. We've all got things in our life we'd like to change, but change requires a *catalyst*. You can't do things the same way you've always done them and expect new results. The first step is always the hardest, from health to love to business. It's never too late to take the first step—and you're going to do it. But before you do, let's talk a little about late bloomers, people who took that first step later in life.

Tokyo's Landlord

Because society loves a good underdog story, you've probably heard about how Michael Jordan was cut from his high school basketball team. You probably also know a little something about JK Rowling, who was 30 when she finished *Harry Potter and the Sorcerer's Stone*, only to have it rejected from 12 publishing houses. You may also know that she received a tiny $3,000 advance from Bloomsbury and that the initial print run was a measly 1,000 copies. (Of course, she's now one of the most successful authors in modern history.) You probably know that Steve Jobs and a dozen other world class entrepreneurs dropped out of college.

You probably don't know about Taikichiro Mori, but in the early 90s he was the richest man in the world. He was Japan's Warren Buffet before Buffet had risen to prominence. He also didn't get started until he was 55 years old. By 1992, he was worth 16 billion dollars, roughly double the net worth of Bill Gates.

Mori was a serene but peculiar man, a quiet genius. He abstained from alcohol and tobacco and worked in a simple black kimono in his office, slightly embarrassed by his international status, but his story begins much earlier. Born in 1904, Mori grew up in the Toranomon neighborhood in Minato ward, Tokyo. Then, Toranomon was a sleepy residential neighborhood criss-crossed by narrow alleys between rows of wooden houses, a scene closer to The Last Samurai than the intense urban sprawl of modern Tokyo.

In his early years, the neighborhood was destroyed not once but twice. The first time was in 1923, when an earthquake devastated much of Tokyo. The second was during World War II, when Tokyo was firebombed. After World War II, Mori taught trade theory at Yokohama City University, where he led a quiet but pleasant life as an academic. Anyone who knew him might've assumed he'd do that until he retired, then perhaps taken up golfing. In 1959, Mori inherited two buildings from his father. He could've sold them. He could have sat on his father's business, letting it stagnate. Instead, he had other ideas—big ones—and he took action.

It took time, but once he'd decided to revolutionize the neighborhood he'd come from, he was not deterred. He had broad redevelopment plans, and he painstakingly convinced the entire neighborhood, both residents and businesses, to support his plan. He bought additional buildings and moved his own employees into the neighborhood. These employees in turn supported his revitalization efforts. Over time, he transformed Tokyo's Minato ward into a slick, modern foothold in the city from which to expand his growing real estate empire. Over time, he became known as Tokyo's landlord—in a good way.

From Landscaping to Big Business

My story's not entirely different. I came out of my college years cocksure and positive I was heading for easy success. I had great grades in college, which I carried forward into business school. After graduation, I applied to a multitude of companies, then sat back and waited for the interview invitations. I was sure they'd be lucky to have me, chomping at the bit to hire.

Well, none wanted me. Each and every one of them turned me down. Instead, I went to work in New York City for my father's landscape design company. Instead of sitting in a leather office chair in a rockstar executive suite, I found myself sweating in the driver's seat of a plant delivery truck, wondering how the hell I'd gotten there. I was humbled.

Over time, the sting to my pride faded, and instead of wondering where I'd screwed up, I started thinking about how to move forward. The first step in everything that came after was in accepting that I wasn't as smart as I thought I was. So I learned everything I could from my father's business—after all, it was a successful one. And when I was sure I'd soaked up as much as I could, I knew it was time to strike out on my own. Forget working for a bunch of companies that didn't want me. Instead, I'd start my own company. At 28 I started from scratch, scrabbling from the bottom to build my first e-commerce business and to mold myself into an Internet marketing authority. I couldn't have done that fresh out of business school. Now I'm thriving as a serial entrepreneur.

Youth and Experience, Effort and Magic

As a species, we tend to romanticize youth. What goes hand in hand with this is a proclivity for associating genius with immaturity. We love a good prodigy almost as much as we love a good underdog. By 1894, on the sunny Spanish coastal city of Málaga, Picasso had already earned himself a reputation as a budding master of his craft—at the age of 13. Mozart was five when he penned his first composition. By the time he was 12, mathematician Blaise Pascal had independently discovered nearly all of Euclid's geometric proofs.

3

But we know better, right? Most of the 21-year-olds I know spend more time crushing beer cans on their heads than writing concertos. It doesn't make them stupid or lazy—it makes them young people who are trying to have fun, and that's fine. Part of the equation of a prodigy story is that the prodigy doesn't usually have to try very hard. Their skill is something more like a superpower than an earned expertise, something for which they seem to just have a preternatural affinity. Like they were born for this.

That's not entirely accurate. Most of the geniuses you know have busted their asses for decades. Somewhere, buried in an old attic, your favorite musician has old cassettes or burned CDs of their early recordings squirreled away, and they're garbage. It's not limited to creative pursuits or business or anything else. Take love, for example: you're roughly twice[1] as likely to get divorced when you marry at 20 than if you wait until 25. In fact, divorce expert Dr. Belinda Hewitt told *The Daily Telegraph* that you're five times[2] more likely to get divorced if you marry in your 20s than if you marry later. It's not hard to imagine why—because our failures matter and because we learn through experience. Our first loves are rarely our last or best loves, and we're not even fully ourselves until later in life. As a species, we continue developing and changing well into adulthood.

The achievements of the prodigies and famous young loves of the world are not greater because they came easy or young. Nor does the fact that they achieved notoriety earlier mean their road to greatness is somehow

---

1. "These Are the Best (and Worst) Ages to Get Married." *Psychology Today.* https://www.psychologytoday.com/us/blog/meet-catch-and-keep/201606/ these- are-the-best-and-worst-ages-get-married.

2. "Does marrying young lead to divorce?" *The Daily Telegraph.* https:// www. dailytelegraph.com.au/lifestyle/stellar/under-30-and-divorced- calling-time-on- failing-marriages-after-tying-the-knot-young/news- story/4431760263c3ca6fd56e1 2431922b5e0.

greater than others—it's just a different path, not a better one. Note also that plenty of young savants burn out early and quickly. So, don't buy into the lie that achievement is a young person's game. For most people, that's not how it works.

Why's that? We all know: because our experiences are valuable. It's all well and good to peak early, but you're left with a narrow worldview and a limited skillset. As I've said before, everything you've experienced in your life up until now—every screw-up, failed relationship, or joyful diversion— they've all shaped who you are. And right now, who you are is a person who's about to change course. Together, over the course of this book, I'm going to help you start thinking about your goals in a different way, and the course of your life is going to change as a result of it.

Ellen Winner is a professor of psychology at Boston College and an expert on gifted youth. In 2015 she told *The New York Times* that "the skill of being a child prodigy is qualitatively different from the 'skill' of being an adult creative genius." I would suggest to you that the same truth extends into early adulthood. Quick success early in life—whether it's in health, love, or career—and sustainable success over the long term require a different set of skills, and the latter's skills are learned and earned, not ingrained. They can be taught. In my experience, I've come up with a solid three-pronged method for thinking about challenges.

Breathe

As you probably expect, when I say "breathe," I'm speaking more figuratively than literally. More than anything, stopping to take a breath is about clarity of mind and purpose, about slowing the hell down for just a minute. I'm not interested in teaching you to succeed in the short term only to have you drop dead of a heart attack at 45 because the pressures of your professional life have become overwhelming. Nor do I want to see someone who's never had a date suddenly start dating a dozen people at once—that's almost as dangerous. We're shooting for sustainable prosperity and, more importantly, happiness. There's no use being successful if it makes you miserable. I'd go

5

so far as to suggest that success and misery cannot co-exist at all—anyone who tells you differently has a shallow view of what success even entails.

There is a little bit of literal breathing to discuss, though. In upcoming chapters, we'll touch on some ways that quick and easy meditation techniques have acted as game-changers for some of the world's most successful individuals.

Once you're in the right headspace, you can take that first concrete step towards facilitating change. We're going to keep talking a lot about that first step, so keep this in the back of your mind going forward.

Focus

I know a lot of serial entrepreneurs, the kind of people with brilliant ideas and no follow-through, armchair Zuckerbergs with no work ethic. They're smart people, but they're constantly spinning their wheels because every week they're chasing a different dream. So once we've taken our first step, we have to make sure the second, third, and fourth are all in the same direction. We can make that easier for ourselves by having a clear plan of action. Other parts of that equation include overcoming our own anxiety about change and failure, avoiding distraction, maximizing productivity, and so on. There are a million tiny ways people sabotage their own best laid plans, and throughout this book I intend to arm you with tools to avoid pitfalls and maximize successes. It doesn't matter whether the goal is to get in shape, to become financially independent, or to find the love of your life—you'll never get there if you don't learn to keep your eye on the ball.

Attack

Our old friend Taikichiro Mori surely knew of Miyamoto Musashi, the greatest samurai swordsman of all time, who himself rose to prominence in his teens, enjoyed a long and fabled run as a master of his craft, and retired to a cave to write down his own wisdom. In regards to battle, he wrote:

*"When you decide to attack, keep calm and dash in quickly,
forestalling the enemy...attack with a feeling of constantly crushing
the enemy, from first to last."*

It's a little brutal, sure, but even Musashi wasn't just talking about fighting—he was talking about crushing obstacles with an undeniable ferocity. This represents the final third of the "Breathe, Focus, Attack" triple-threat. Once you're clear on your goal and sure of the way forward, there's no room for hesitation. You have to push forward with determination, starting strong and finishing strong, until the job's done. Going forward, we'll talk about how to avoid burnout, how to harness the support of friends and family, and how to turn all that determination and intent into real results.

This book is for the late bloomers, the outcasts, the scrappy underdogs—in short, it's for most of us. So, let's get started.

1) Identify a goal.

You're probably reading this book with a particular challenge in mind. There's probably one area of you're life you'd most like to improve. In time, I sincerely hope you'll improve *every* area of your life, but it's helpful to break down big tasks into smaller, more manageable ones. So, identify the area of your life where you'd like to see a change. Then, narrow it down to one actionable goal within that area. So, something like "I want to make more money" is too general. "I want to get a promotion at work" is better. For our purposes, you need a goal you can see. Write it down.

_____

_____

_____

2) Identify the first step.

You don't have to have the whole path to success mapped out yet. For now, we only need to focus on the first step. After all, that's the hardest and most important one, and it's the one that 95% of people never take. That's not you—not anymore. You don't have to actually *take* this step yet. For now it's enough to have it in your head. Let's take our promotion example: you'd have to ask your boss, of course, but before that meeting it would be a good idea to prepare, to have a well-structured argument for why you deserve the raise. This might include numbers reflecting your productivity and efficiency or a short list of some of your achievements on the job. For you and your goal, what's the first step?

_____

_____

_____

Chapter Two:

Learn to Say "No"

"SAY YES!" IT'S A MANTRA to some. On its surface, the philosophy makes plenty of sense: be open to new ideas and experiences, grasp chances to try new things and participate in projects bigger than yourself. Here's the thing: it's bullshit.

I suppose it's fine if your goal is to experience a lot of different things and have little to show for it at the end. If your long-term goal itself is to say "yes", then by all means, say "yes." But if you want to build something, you have to understand that you have a limited amount of time at your disposal and to start guarding it jealously.

Among people who do actually try to do something with their lives, one of the things that separate those who succeed from those who fail is how much of their own time they squander. This is an especially easy trap in that maximum productivity can look a lot like being extraordinarily busy—just look at how many people proudly use the hashtag #nosleep on social media in the midst of all-night work binges.

Why brag about creating a lifestyle for yourself in which you have no time? Isn't the whole point to be able to expend our energy how we want to, to gain freedom from the rat race?

There's a shortcut to reclaiming an awful lot of your time: saying "no" more often. Often our natural inclination is to think it's rude to say "no," but that's a habit that it's time to unlearn.

The Death of OpenDoc

Steve Jobs loved saying "no." He loved it so much and believed in the power of refusal to such a degree that every day he asked Jony Ive how many times he'd said "no" that day. He did it to the point that Ive affectionately admitted that it was "patronizing." Jony Ive is Apple's Chief Design Officer, and he's responsible for the design of the 700 million iPhones in use today, so it's safe to say the guy knows a thing or two about getting things done.

Let's back up for those not intimately acquainted with Steve Jobs's biography, because it's incredible. Jobs co-founded Apple at 21 and was a millionaire by 23. Soon after he recruited the CEO of Pepsi-Cola, John Sculley, to be Apple's new CEO. In fact, he famously poached him by asking, "Do you want to sell sugar water for the rest of your life, or do you want to come with me and change the world?" Three years later, the first Mac computer was launched. The reviews were glowing, but the sales weren't. Jobs's general rebel attitude and management style also contributed to his fraying relationship with the company board. His team was housed in its own building, where he flew a pirate flag. "It's better to be a pirate than to be in the Navy," he said. He was passionate, and he didn't give a damn if it rubbed people the wrong way. He picked fights. He was demanding. He pushed his team to greatness, but it wore on them, and from the outside not everyone liked the way it looked.

So, at age 30, Steve Jobs was fired. He wasn't quietly let go. John Sculley led the charge (with the backing of the board) and humiliatingly and very publicly ousted Jobs from his own company.

Jobs spent the next few months in a tailspin, unsure of what to do next, even kicking around the idea of entering politics or becoming an astronaut. Instead, he founded two new companies: NeXT and Pixar. (That's right, the same Pixar that's responsible for every animated blockbuster you've ever seen a commercial for.)

The king had fallen, but he was clawing his way back up. He described this period as exceptionally freeing. Jobs said that getting fired had "replaced the heaviness of being successful with the lightness of being a beginner again," and that this had rekindled his inner creativity. During this period, he also learned how to be a businessman—not just a creative.

Meanwhile, Apple was struggling. In 1996, they acquired NeXT, meaning Jobs once again worked for the company he'd founded. It didn't take long for him to rise to the top once again, and soon he was CEO.

By this time, Jobs had learned the power of saying "no". Apple engineers were working hard on a software product called OpenDoc, and Jobs killed it almost immediately upon his return. He described it as "shooting [the project] in the head." He killed it, he claimed, because of a lack of company focus. Apple had all these brilliant people running around doing dozens of brilliant things at once, and all of those things were new and interesting and potential money-makers. The problem was that they were different, and the company couldn't do everything at once. Jobs's strategy—and it's one we should probably emulate—was to focus on a few things at a time and do them better than anyone else. Speaking to the company's developers, he explained:

> "What happened was, you look at the farm that's been created, with all these different animals going in different directions, and it doesn't add up. The total is less than the sum of the parts. And so we had to decide: What are the fundamental directions we're going in? And what makes sense and what doesn't? And there were a bunch of things that didn't. And micro-cosmically they might have made sense; macro-cosmically they made no sense.
>
> When you think about focusing, you think, well, focusing is about saying yes. No. Focusing is about saying no."

11

Breathe: Looks Can Be Deceiving

Take a breath. Saying "no" isn't going to wreck your life. You're not going to hurt people's feelings. You're not going to miss out on critical opportunities. By the end of this chapter, you'll know how to refuse gracefully and to develop laser-like focus.

Jobs pointed out something critical: When you're saying no, often you'll be saying it to things that look like good opportunities. Maybe they actually *are* good opportunities. They're not just for you—at least not right now. It's easy to say "no" to things that don't interest you. It's much harder to say "no" to things that are tempting: ideas that you know are good, projects that excite you, or relationships that are new and intriguing. Discerning which opportunities are truly worthwhile is a skill that may take some trial and error to develop, but the most important thing for you right now is to start cultivating a mindset in which you respect your own time and understand that it's a limited resource. Stop wasting your own time, and stop letting others waste it for you.

Decide to do things with intention. One of the biggest differences between people who are good at achieving their goals and people who aren't is that the former tend to grasp intentionality in a different way. They do things deliberately, not arbitrarily, and they make it a habit, whether it's in their work, their love life, or their approach to their own health and wellness. And guess what? You'll hear me say it a million times, but once you make this a habit, it becomes easy. Anyone can train themselves in this way. The more you say "no" and the more you choose to laser-focus your energy, the easier it becomes.

Do you sometimes feel like obligations have piled up to the point that you're spread thin? Are you used to the weight of those obligations just sort of sitting in the back of your mind? Take a moment to imagine what it would be like if you had fewer entanglements. Imagine how it would feel to be able to think about what's right in front of you instead of worrying about the other things you'll need to take care of later, or tomorrow, or next week.

After you read this paragraph, put the book down. Take a deep breath. Let yourself relax. Then picture what your life will be like when you're free to focus your time and energy on the stuff you really should be doing and the people who really matter. Once you can see it, decide you're going to start taking steps in that direction. Then pick the book back up, because we're going to get started.

Focus: How to Say No Gracefully

Before you can take action, you need to focus in on the proper way to do it. You may know Tim Ferriss, author of *Tribe of Mentors* and *The 4-Hour Workweek*. When writing *Tribe of Mentors*, Ferris asked dozens and dozens of successful people to lend him some life advice for the book, and many turned him down. What's interesting here is not that they declined—we've already discussed all the reasons why they'd do that—but *how* they declined. For Ferris, the similarities between the rejection letters were striking, both in their similarity and in their effectiveness. They were direct and to the point, but they were also respectful, even kind. Each had a similar structure:

1) Personal acknowledgment.

It's not rocket science: people want to think you're not just giving them a kneejerk brush-off. A simple sentence or two that in some way demonstrates that you're paying attention to the correspondent and their request goes a long way towards taking the sting off of saying no.

Example: *"Hey, Mark! Thanks for getting in touch and asking me to do an interview for your podcast. I listened to the latest episode on my drive to the office today, and it was great."*

2) Telling them that you've got too much on your plate.

Chances are, you're saying no because you're short on time, not because the correspondent is a jerk or because their pitch is dumb, so it's enough to just tell them that you're already overcommitted as it is. People like

13

being spoken to directly and honestly. That's how friends talk to one another.

Example: *"Unfortunately, I'm going to have to pass, at least for now. I'm honored that you'd ask, but the fact of the matter is that I'm covered up with other responsibilities right now."*

3) <u>Explanation that you have to focus on your own priorities right now.</u>
People can sympathize with the feeling of being stretched thin, and it's fair game to explain that you simply have to keep your eye on the ball right now.

Example: *"I always want to jump on every opportunity that comes my way, by lately I'm finding that if I don't carve out some time for myself I'll never get my own projects finished."*

4) <u>Explanation of what those priorities actually are.</u>
People sympathize even better if you tell them a little about what those priorities are. You don't have to give them your whole life story, but specifics help.

Example: *"I'm actually writing a book called* Breathe, Focus, Attack, *and the deadline from my editor is right around the corner."*

5) <u>Explanation of why this prior commitment is very important right now.</u>
On occasion, people will still think you're making a mistake, because their opportunity is clearly more important than whatever you're doing. This has happened to me before. "I understand where you're coming from," they'll say. "But I would hate for you to regret not getting involved down the line." So far, they've never been right.

Example: *"I've wanted to write a book pretty much my whole life, so it's a dream come true, and I want to focus all of my energy on doing it as well as I can."*

> 6) Tell them you have a general policy of not taking on any new responsibilities at this time.

Basically a classic "it's not you, it's me" line.

Example: *"As such, at this time I'm not taking on any new obligations. Again, I really appreciate you reaching out about it, and I hope we get to collaborate on something in the future."*

Put all of this together, and you've got yourself a compact little one-paragraph response that will protect your time whilst keeping you classy and thoughtful. Not too shabby. These same basic principles can be applied to real-life interactions just as easily, and obviously they don't have to be work-related. Think about the ways that your social life may also encroach on itself. You only get one Saturday night a week, after all. Are you the kind of person who often finds themself attending events out of a sense of obligation, instead of spending that time the way you'd really like to or with the people you'd really like to? Well, buckle up, because it's time to start turning people down.

Attack: Part 1 — Protect Your Time

Identify what you most think you should truly be doing. The thing that your soul tells you is your calling, the thing you were born to do. Now, identify the responsibilities in your life right now that are keeping you from spending more time on that. If you don't protect your own time, nobody will, and you may find it slipping away little by little.

_____
_____
_____
_____

_____

_____

_____

_____

_____

Attack: Part 2 — Mind Map

This is the first mind map you'll be creating as a part of going through this book, but it's not going to be the last. I've found them enormously helpful in terms of jumpstarting my own creativity and getting information out of my head. All mind maps share the same structure, but there are few rules here. Basically, we're listing out items and their relationships but in a more fluid and natural way than a simple list. As an example, I might start my map with a single concept in a circle on the center of the page. For this chapter, it's going to be:

The whole point of this chapter is that time is a limited resource. It's a precious currency, and you can't spend it on multiple things at once. As such, wrangling my time use and better controlling my obligations means identifying roadblocks that stand in my way. These might be my own habits, or they might be the result of saying "yes" to things *other* people want me to do that I shouldn't be doing. So far, not exactly complicated, right? Next, I'll add sub-categories as offshoots from that central concept:

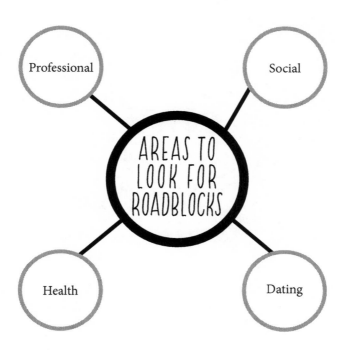

You see where this is going, right? I've identified four major areas of my life that are important to me, areas where I'm happy but want to improve even further. One of the major advantages of this brainstorming method is that expressing the ideas visually like this allows you to see relationships and make comparisons in a way you otherwise wouldn't. You may not be used to writing things out at all, but bear with me, sincerely try this out, and I think you'll be pleasantly surprised. Let's say I drill down another level:

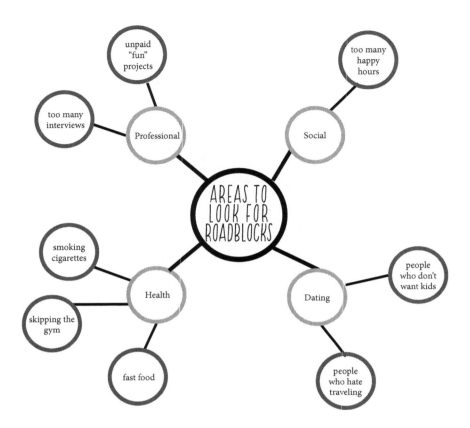

Now I'm getting into specific roadblocks that are keeping me from achieving as much as I could in each of these areas. At a glance, it looks like there are more hurdles to clear in the "Health" arena than "Social." I'm not that off-base in that area of my life, though perhaps instead of going to happy hour after work, I could spend some of that time going to the gym more often—I could eliminate two roadblocks in one swipe! Remember, everything's a trade-off. Every time I'm hanging out at the bar, I'm not doing something else. There has to be some balance. As for dating? Let's assume I'm trying to find the person I'll spend the rest of my life with. Well, I've identified two dealbreakers: I can't imagine being married to someone who wouldn't travel the world with me, and I'm sure I want children one day. If that's true, I should say "no" to dating people who don't align with that. No matter how beautiful she is, if I go out with her, I'm wasting her time and mine.

Health is no different, and at a glance it looks like I've got further to go in this area of my life than in any of the others. I might not even have recognized it until now, seeing it on paper. Every time I eat a meal or choose a drink or undertake some form of exercise, I'm doing that to the exclusion of something else. For the purposes of our example let's say I'm trying to generally live a healthier lifestyle—well, I should say "no" to taking too many days off of exercise, eating any fast food, and smoking the occasional cigarette. Every time I say "no" to one of these things, I'm focusing on a decision that will benefit my end goal. And after saying "no" to fast food for a little while, for example, it will become easier to say "yes" to a healthy lunch and harder to say "yes" to an unhealthy one.

You get the picture. If we're being real about it, mind mapping may seem like a silly activity at first, but if you put your ass in a chair, whip out a notebook, and try it out, you'll find that your subconscious finds its way onto the page. I'd encourage you to try these for several subjects as the book goes on.

Chapter Three:

Friends

I'D LIKE TO KICK THIS CHAPTER off by making an assertion: most average people don't consciously choose the people they surround themselves with. Without thinking too much about it, they may naturally gravitate towards people they feel comfortable around, and then circumstance and proximity sprinkle a few more people into the mix. People settle into routines. As they get older, they often stop seeking out new and different relationships altogether. It's easy to become complacent and content with the status quo, even in terms of who we hang out with.

People with above-average success do most things with above-average intentionality, which includes consciously choosing the people they surround themselves with. Studies have suggested that people with strong, healthy friendships experience less stress, recover from setbacks more quickly, and achieve more.

High-profile examples of the opposite abound. Celebrities who slip into addiction often surround themselves with people who facilitate bad choices and discourage recovery. Or take, for example, major scandals in the business world. Remember Enron? Friendships and business relationships at the executive level among toxic individuals created a culture of dishonesty and greed, and the results speak for themselves: 11 executives were indicted, and the company's shareholders lost $74 billion. The effects trickled down to the rank and file as well, with tens of thousands of employees losing their jobs and pensions. We should always be striving to surround ourselves with people who bring out the best in us, not the worst, but sometimes it's easier said than done. Sometimes, it's not clear which is which.

Sociological research suggests that happiness, sadness, and other emotions spread through social groups similar to the way viruses do. A study from the Royal Society of London, for example, found that for every positively-minded person you keep in your life, your own likelihood of exhibiting a positive outlook increases by 11%. The opposite is also true but even harsher: for each unhappy person you have a relationship with, your chance of becoming unhappy doubles.[3]

All along, I've been trying to encourage you to be more proactive and less reactive, to take tangible steps towards creating the life you want for yourself. A vital part of that equation isn't about you at all—it's about who your friends are.

Takers and Toxic Relationships

What is a toxic relationship? Simply put, it's a relationship that is harmful to one of the parties involved. Healthy relationships involve give and take, with both friends propping each other up, supporting one another, and helping in times of need. The toxic individual tends to be more self-centered and manipulative in their dealings with others, though they may go their entire lives without ever realizing it. In fact, toxic people *usually* don't know they're toxic. That requires both a self-awareness and an empathy towards others that they lack. They're too worried about themselves for it to occur to them that maybe there's something you need out of the friendship that they're not

---

3. "Emotions as infectious diseases in a large social network: the SISa model." Proceedings of the Royal Society of London B: Biological Sciences. http://rspb. royalsocietypublishing.org/content/277/1701/3827.short

giving you. Toxic relationships come in all shapes and sizes and can extend beyond friendships—you might have a toxic boss, parent, or spouse.

How Do You Know If You're in a Toxic Relationship?

Judge it by its fruit. If the friendship has more negative than positive effects in your life, the odds are good that it's bringing you down. Honest answers to the following questions might provide some clarity:

1. Do you feel emotionally drained after dealing with this person?

2. When you know you're going to spend time with this person, do you feel happy or apprehensive?

3. Do you worry about this person interacting with other people you know?

4. Do you feel that you have to keep your guard up when you're around them?

5. Have this person's actions caused negative consequences in *your* life?

6. Do they lie or manipulate often?

7. Does their presence in your life *add* problems to your life or *remove* them?

What Can You Do If You're in a Toxic Relationship?

You've got three options:

1) You can stay in the relationship as-is. This is rarely the right option. New results require new circumstances, right? When people stay in relationships that are bad for them—whether they're social, romantic, or professional—it's often because they feel guilty exiting them. Don't. Sometimes you have to prioritize your mental and emotional health. You have to take care of yourself and protect yourself in order to thrive. If it feels rude or mean to willingly distance yourself from a toxic friend, just remind yourself that they are doing you harm_through their behavior, and by not changing something about the dynamic you're enabling them.

2) You can attempt to repair the relationship. This probably means talking with the toxic friend about their behavior. Remember, they probably don't realize they're a bad friend. Unfortunately, many people will become defensive when confronted with concerns, especially if they're the self-centered type—they may try to shift the conversation to the ways *you* have wronged *them*. Regardless, if you go this route, don't let it become an argument. Go into this conversation with a clear objective in mind. *For our friendship to work, [Insert Thing] needs to change.* If it's clear the change won't happen, you already know you're going to move on or limit your interaction with that person, so there's no sense in allowing further negativity. On the other hand, some people will make a sincere attempt to change the dynamic of your relationship, which can be wonderful. In this case, ask yourself: what are your bottom lines? What behavior do they *have* to change for you to stick it out?

3) You can exit the friendship. If a relationship is sucking you dry and piling on challenges in your life as opposed to enriching it, you may be better off just moving on. Don't think of it is as ending a friendship—think of it as identifying who your real friends actually are. Some people choose to simply taper off contact over time, allowing the relationship to fizzle and avoiding drama. People grow apart all the time. It's a natural part of life. Think back to Chapter 2. By saying "no" to friendships that are holding you back, you free yourself up to say "yes" to new friendships that make you stronger, better, and happier.

Friends With Benefits

We've spent a few pages talking about ridding yourself of people who only drag you down, but there's a brighter side. Friends, loved ones, and professional relationships can turbocharge your success in ways few other things can. We all know what "friends with benefits" are—well, all healthy friendships have a multitude of benefits, some of which you may not know.

- That trite-sounding platitude about how "attitudes are contagious?" It's true. Surrounding yourself with optimistic, positive people increases those traits in your own mind.

- Better health. People with good friends not only suffer a lower incidence of mental health issues; there's also a link to greater general physical health, including lower rates of cardiovascular disease. This may be due to a lower general level of stress, which is in and of itself invaluable.

- Friends provide a valuable sounding board. They'll give honest feedback about your ideas, suggest ways to improve, and give you a kick in the backside when you need it.

- Friends can provide logistical support. Friends come with their own sets of skills, connections, and resources, meaning they can provide all kinds of support in making your plans become a reality.

- Friends act as a safety net. Bigger successes also often mean bigger challenges and responsibilities. It becomes more important than ever to know that a good group of true friends has your back.

- Friends lead to friends. The larger your social circle grows, the more influence you gain in other areas of your life. And friends introduce you to more friends.

The Five Types of Friends Successful People Have

Friends come in all shapes. Average people often seek out relationships simply based on unexamined impulses about whether they "like" someone, which is a vague enough notion in and of itself. And in most cases, when we say we "like" someone, what we really mean is that we like how they make us *feel.* Their presence puts us at ease or makes us laugh or makes us feel secure. That gains you one type of friend—what I'll call a "pal" below. But not all friends are like that, and some friendships can be beneficial to you because they challenge you, push you to be your best self, educate you, or provide you opportunities to give back.

The Pals. This is the most stereotypical picture of a friend people usually have—the people you hang out with casually, the crew you join on Saturday nights, the people who attend parties you throw. Friends can be "pals" and other types of friends at the same time, but take care not to let other types of relationships (like business relationships) affect relationships that started as "pals."

The Mentors. Mentorship is something of a hallowed new tradition in entrepreneurial circles, but for those just finding their professional legs, the term may sound foreign. We all know, of course, that a mentor is a more experienced individual that takes a long-term interest in fostering your growth. Be on the lookout for potential mentors as you grow. This might be a boss, a professor, a coach, or simply an acquaintance whose success and style you admire. You'd be surprised how willing people are to take on a mentor role in your life, as well as how generous they'll be with their time and knowledge. Many successful people learned valuable lessons along the way from mentors themselves, so they're apt to help set the next generation up for success. Additionally, successful and driven people are often passionate about what it is they do, so they may really enjoy teaching others.

The Pupils. Likewise, also look for opportunities to pass on the things *you* know to people who share an interest. Investing time in people is rewarding in its own right. Teaching others also solidifies and sharpens your own knowledge. In the medical world, the traditional framework for surgical training is to "See One, Do One, Teach One." That is to say that watching someone else do a procedure lays the groundwork, and doing one yourself demonstrates basic proficiency. But when you successfully teach the procedure to another person, you know your understanding of the concepts is complete. You know *why* and *how* the treatment works—not just how to perform the steps. The same is true in all areas of life. Finally, good pupils tend to become better contemporaries. When you help train someone up to the point that they themselves become successful, those people can become valuable and loyal connections.

The Partners. This primarily applies to business, but some relationships chiefly provide strategic benefits. Whether you "like" the friend in question is secondary. You may have differences of opinion with someone but still share common business goals and philosophies—that's a friend of a different stripe, but it's still one to seek out. This is a common mistake. With strategic partners, it's not necessarily important how they make you feel or whether you enjoy their presence—it's whether your friendship with them advances your common goals.

The Virtual Acquaintances. Today, the value of virtual acquaintances— "Internet friends"—can't really be understated. Most of us spend all day long walking around with a computer in our pockets that can reach millions of people in the blink of an eye. It's a remarkable thing. When the millionaires of your grandparents' generation were making their fortunes, they didn't have the Internet to leverage as a source of knowledge and connection, but you do. All manner of online communities exist that allow for the sharing of knowledge, building connections, and direct collaboration. With a minimum time investment, the Internet can help you grow your social circle exponentially.

Breathe: Identify Your Friendships

The time to complacently drift through social circles is over. It's time to take a moment to step back and reflect on the people around you. Think back again to Chapter 2, and remember that when you're saying "yes" to someone, you're effectively saying "no" to someone else. Why? Because you've got limited time, but you've also got limited space in your brain.

What do I mean by that? There's a limit to the number of meaningful relationships any of us can maintain, and there may even be a physiological mechanism that helps determine it. There's a British anthropologist and evolutionary psychologist by the name of Robin Dunbar for whom an idea is named: Dunbar's Number. The quick and dirty version is this: Dunbar studied brain development and social behavior in monkeys, and he discovered a correlation between the brain size of monkeys and the size of the social groups they formed. Monkeys with bigger brains—smarter species of monkeys—were able to maintain larger social groups. Social groups in primates self-correct; if the population of a given troop gets too big, the monkeys begin to have problems. They can't feed everyone, they get into fights, and things get generally messy. Eventually, Dunbar's team was able to predict monkey group size by looking only at their brains. Without any other knowledge about a particular monkey species, they could measure the size of its brain and accurately predict the approximate population of that monkey's community.

Can you guess where this is going? Applying the same ideas to human brains and extrapolating the results gets you a theoretical number of how many people the average human should be able to maintain stable relationships with. That number falls between 100 and 250, but it's usually stated as being 150.

Of course, this is all a little oversimplified, and the theories surrounding it go into much more depth, but as a thought experiment it's useful. You've got a social bubble around you, and only so many people can fit in it at once. If that's the case, shouldn't you be more aware of who is in it?

Take a few minutes to just reflect on the composition of your social circle. Who are the people that have the strongest day-to-day impact on your life? Are any of them particularly negative or particularly positive influences? Are there any relationships that you feel, perhaps on some gut level, could be more beneficial to you if you invested more time and energy into them? What would your ideal friend circle look like? The healthiest, happiest version of your social life? What concrete changes can you make to make it a reality?

Focus:

Maybe upon reflection, you're realizing most of your friends are pals that you've semi-randomly accumulated along the way.

The opposite case can also occur. If all of your friends are facilitated through business, or if most of your friends are online, you may benefit from more face-to-face "pal" activity. Balance is key. Decide which types of friendships you should cultivate more of.

Attack: Diversify Your Friend Portfolio

Having decided which types of friendships you'd like to further develop, it's time to put a plan into action. For each type of friend you might want more of, there's a different action step below.

Pals: If you want to make some more casual friends, convert acquaintances or join a social activity. Can you think of some people you've met that you think could become better friends? Get in touch with them now. Organize a get-together for dinner or drinks. If you'd like to meet some totally new people, try joining an event related to a hobby or interest that meets in your area. If you're in a large enough town, there are probably things like running/biking clubs, gaming groups, and even entrepreneurial meet-ups available to you. You just have to take a minute to look for them. Make a plan and schedule an activity for this week.

Mentors: Think of some people—preferably in your city—who are where you want to be. It doesn't matter if you have a pre-existing social connection to them or not. Look up their e-mail, and if you can find it, drop them a line. Tell them that you admire their work and are yourself trying to make a name in the same field. Ask them a question or two. This opening salvo can easily lead to a larger conversation and may plant the seeds for a long and fruitful friendship.

Pupils: If you're a boss, are there people who work for you that have shown a sincere interest in the work that you might cultivate? If so, make a plan to engineer a sit-down conversation with them this week. Find out what makes them tick. Ask them what their long-term goals are. Everyone's motivations at work are different, and if you know theirs, you can learn how to best help them succeed. Alternatively, do some research on volunteer opportunities in to your community, programs in which you can pass on your time and knowledge.

Partners: Way back in the beginning of this book, we acknowledged the fact that most readers probably have a long-term over-arching goal they're working towards. With that in mind, what kind of person would make a valuable ally in achieving that goal? If you're starting a business, for example, you might possess a strong strategic mind but lack a creative background— in that case, forging a relationship with a talented creative professional could be breathe some real life into your projects. Another example: if your goal is to live a healthier lifestyle, you might reach out to someone you know who's in great shape and ask if you can work out with them. Regardless of your specific situation, think of someone whose goals align with your own, then take a concrete step and reach out to them. Not tomorrow, not next week. Right now, before moving on to the next chapter.

Virtual Acquaintances: Again, what's your primary Big Goal right now? Seek out and join at least one online community related to that goal. Good places to start might be Facebook groups or Subreddit communities.

In Closing

They say you are the company you keep, and there's probably some truth to that. And I know I've already said it, but if you do the same things you've always done, you'll get the same results you always have. By phasing out toxic relationships and cultivating and diversifying healthy ones, you'll see improvements in every area of your life.

Chapter Four:

What to Say Yes To

IMAGINE YOU'RE IN A PUBLIC PLACE—you can choose for yourself where—
and someone suddenly yells "bomb!" You can see it right there in the middle
of the room, and sure enough, it looks like a bomb: there's a watch attached
to what looks like packed explosives, connected by colored wires, just like
something out of *Die Hard*. There's a timer counting down from 30 seconds.
Suddenly, a guy appears amidst the crowd and says, "Stand back, I've got this
covered!" He's rolling up his sleeves. He's going to try to defuse it.

"So are you, like, some kind of bomb squad guy?" you ask.

"No," he says. "It's okay, though."

"So then you must be ex-military."

He's starting to look annoyed now. "No, but I'm very smart. And I'm
a nice guy. I never forget birthdays, I always pay my taxes, and I'm a great
listener."

You ask, "How does any of that matter now? Can you defuse the damn
bomb or not?"

He's baffled and aggravated. "What's your problem?" he asks. "Aren't you
listening to me? Why are you being so close-minded? Don't you care about
my good qualities?"

Of course you don't. In this moment, all you care about is whether or not
he can fix the problem at hand. Do you want this guy attempting to disarm
the bomb? Probably not. This is similar to a scenario proposed by writer

David Wong in an article for Cracked.com[4], and the point being illustrated is this: it doesn't matter what great qualities you think you have. *What matters is what you do with them.* The world is full of problems waiting to be solved, and in a practical and brutal sense, you matter about as much as you can solve them.

When you hear someone lamenting that they're smart and hard-working but they just can't seem to get ahead professionally, it's because they're not utilizing those traits. When "nice guys" just can't get a date, it's because women don't cares if they're nice or not—they care about how that niceness manifests through action. They care about what their prospective date bring to the table and how their presence enriches their life. Lots of people are nice to pretty girls. It's not special. So don't ask yourself, how come I can't own a successful company? Ask yourself, what things do people who own a successful company do that I'm not doing? Don't ask why you can't find a loving partner. Ask how you can become the kind of person who has a healthy dating life. See the difference?

In this chapter, there are two kinds of things to say "yes" to—the big ones and little ones. The macro and the micro. The big thing to say yes to is your primary purpose in life. The little things are the things that get you closer to achieving that purpose.

That probably means learning new habits and skills. It's like we forget at some point in our adulthoods that we can still do that. You can definitely teach old dogs new tricks. You can learn new languages, musical instruments, and professional skills just as easily as you could when you were younger, but for whatever reason most of us forget. It probably has something to do with the way society structures us to think about education: when you're a kid, you go to school. At some point, usually after high school or college, it's time to "enter the real world," at which point you're supposed to become concerned with adult responsibilities. Of course, those first 18 years of your

---

4. Wong, David. "6 Harsh Truths That Will Make You a Better Person." http://www.cracked.com/blog/6-harsh-truths-that-will-make-you-better-person.

life are as "real" as any other, and becoming an adult doesn't mean it's time to stop learning. So how do you find your true purpose? I subscribe to the Venn diagram below:

'X' marks the spot. The best version of you doing the best work you can do in life lies at the intersection of what you love, what you're good at, what you can get paid for, and what the world needs. Someone may be willing to pay you for something you're great at, and that will make a great job—but if you don't love it, it's just a paycheck. Or you may find something you're passionate about that's for a good cause, but if you can't monetize it, it won't ever be the way you pay your bills. There's no rule that says your profession has to also be your mission, of course. You can work a 9-to-5, then come home and pursue your passion to your heart's content. But if you can find that sweet spot where you're doing what you love, that thing benefits others, and you're making money, everything will click into place.

I can't tell you what that looks like for your life. Nobody can. But think about the diagram, take a real inventory of your interests and talents, and see what ideas emerge. When you find that one activity where everything comes together, say yes to it. That's your life's greatest yes.

Making that purpose a reality involves a saying yes to a lot of other, smaller good habits along the way, just as it involves saying no to things that steer you off course.

How to Build New Habits

It's all well and good to decide you want to say yes to some new and exciting venture. How do you actually do it? Saying yes is in some ways the easy part. People living mediocre lives do it all the time. *I'm going to write a book this summer. I'm going to get in shape, starting this week. I'm going to finally start my own business.* Following through is the hard part. And, of course, the fear of failing at whatever the endeavor is can either stop someone from ever making a real effort or become a self-fulfilling prophecy. So how do we avoid this fate? It's simple: **rig the game.** Set the bar low so that you can succeed more easily, and you'll naturally start to develop a habit of success. Perhaps you want to run a marathon, for example. Don't try to force yourself to run 10 miles a day in the lead-up. At first, maybe you just shoot for one mile on Monday, Wednesday, and Friday. Soon, that thrice-weekly run will become a part of your normal routine, and your natural inclination will be to avoid skipping it, not to avoid doing it. In this way, you train your brain. After a few weeks, you can start making your runs longer. You have to learn to crawl before you can run, and this is also something we seem to forget as we get older. We're comfortable being beginners when we're younger—it's a state we often find ourselves in. As we get older, we cling more fiercely to our comfort zones. When we hit goals, even if intellectually we know we've set the bar low, our dopamine spikes. Dopamine is the "feel-good neurotransmitter," the same chemical the brain releases when you eat something delicious or get a kiss from a loved one. Whenever your brain doses itself with dopamine, it wants to repeat the behavior that caused the reaction. So, the more you succeed, the more your brain pushes you to do the same thing. That's important, because as a general rule the human brain favors routine over new things, even when those routines are objectively not in your best interest. So, to succeed we want to retrain the brain.

There *is* one key requirement to making this strategy work: you have to have goals. Keep them easily attainable at first, but have them.

The biological side of all of this goes deeper still. According to a 2016 study in *Neuron*, goals and habits are stored in different areas of the brain. The orbitofrontal cortex is responsible for converting *things you wish you did* into *things you naturally want to do*. You can help your endocannaboid system along by giving it a **specific context** for the new habit.[5] So, in the case of our marathon example, you'll develop the running habit more quickly if you always run after work, or always run at 6:00 AM. Attach the new habit to any sort of specific context, and it will solidify more quickly.

There's another, secondary strategy to employ here, too: **break big challenges down into little ones.** The thought of writing an entire book can be overwhelming, so don't think about writing an entire book. Think about writing the first chapter. The week after that, you can worry about the next chapter, then the next. Focus on the task immediately in front of you, and as long as you put one foot in front of the other and keep on going, you'll succeed.

---

5. Gremel, Christina. M, *et al.* "Endocannabinoid Modulation of Orbitostriatal Circuits Gates Habit Formation." *Neuron. https://www.cell.com/neuron/fulltext/ S0896-6273%2816%2930157-X#%20.*

Good Examples of Things to Say Yes To

Again, I'm talking about the sorts of everyday success-building habits to say "yes" to that get you to your bigger "yes"—your ultimate mission. As I've said, the brain loves routine and hates novelty, and paradoxically that's bad for us, even on a chemical level (new and novel experiences increase seratonin production, which helps us feel happy and fulfilled.) Below is a casual list of 10 things that you should almost always say yes to.

- Meeting new people and inviting them to hang out.

- Reading. It's almost never a bad time to be reading.

- Turning off your devices and leaving them off for a while.

- Accepting help, whether it's for something big, or in the workplace, or when an employee at a store asks you if you need help finding something.

- Decluttering your life, including throwing out old knick-knacks or donating clothing you never wear anymore.

- Catching up with old friends.

- Going to bed extra early every once in a while.

- Try out a new hobby you've always been interested in.

- Hand-writing letters and cards.

- Doing something you've never done before.

Breathe: Time Out For Meditation

This time, I'm going to suggest you literally focus on your breathing. Saying "yes" to meditation is something a startling number of successful people do. I've mentioned Tim Ferris's excellent *Tribe of Mentors* already—well, in the course of interviewing over 200 successful people, one unexpected tidbit that Ferris learned is that over 80% of them meditated. It didn't matter if they were a professional athlete, millionaire entrepreneur, or gifted artist.

Mindfulness is one of the best kept secrets of the business world, which is why you'll find meditation spaces on numerous Silicon Valley campuses. It probably won't surprise you to learn that our revered Steve Jobs was into meditation, too. In fact, he was into meditation before it was cool. He traveled to India in 1974, and after he got a taste for the contemplative life transformed it into an ongoing part of his professional life. He had this to say about it:

> "If you just sit and observe, you will see how restless your mind is. If you try to calm it, it only makes it worse, but over time it does calm, and when it does, there's room to hear more subtle things—that's when your intuition starts to blossom and you start to see things more clearly and be in the present."

If you take a glass of the muddiest river water you can find, set it down on a counter, and leave it, what happens? It settles. In fact, it begins to settle almost immediately. The dirt and grime that seem to define the water sink to the bottom of the glass, and what's left is clear, sparkling water—clarity is restored. The mind works the same way. Taking even just a few minutes to sit still and allow the brain to settle has remarkable benefits.

When we meditate regularly, we also learn to be more aware of the interactions between mind, body, and emotion, seeing the ways in which they affect each other. We see how our negative emotions feed physical responses—increased heartrate, flushing of the face, etc.—and how this in turn re-feeds the negative emotion, creating a biofeedback loop that's hard to shake. Simply learning to be aware in the moment when these things are happening creates a sense of space between our experience of emotions and our need to react to them. We've talked about how anxiety, for example, can paralyze people into inaction. Worrying about the potential negative consequences of taking a risk can keep people from ever taking the risk, and that's how life becomes stagnant. With routine meditation, we can train ourselves to see an emotional like anxiety as less like an overwhelming sense of being and more like traffic passing by our field of vision. We can note that it's coming and watch it go without allowing it to take hold.

Meditation is a skill and a habit, and hopefully the previous section has prepared you to take that on. There's really no wrong way to meditate, but there are an infinite number of useful resources on the subject. These days, one of the most popular ways to help build the habit is through meditation apps. Headspace, Calm, and Insight Timer are among the more popular ones as of 2018.

Start off slow. Maybe just try five minutes at a time. Surely you can find five minutes a day, right? Again, attach it to a specific context to solidify the habit. You might always do it right after taking your morning shower or right after you eat lunch, for example. It's useful to do it closer to the beginning of your day, so you can carry that clarity forward.

Focus: Give it a Try

I do recommend doing some research or trying a meditation app, but for the sake of giving it a try, for the first few days you can just do this:

- Set a timer for the length of time you want to sit. Do this so you don't feel compelled to look at the time to see how long you've been sitting.

- Sit down in a chair or on the floor in any posture that feels comfortable. Try to avoid lying down in bed.

- Take just a moment to be aware of the space around you—any smells or sounds that jump out to you. Note also the way your body feels: the points of contact between your body and the chair, any tension in the muscles, etc.

- Either close your eyes or leave them partially opened with a "soft focus," not looking at anything in particular.

- Focus on the breath. Breathe in through the nose and out through the mouth, loud enough that you can hear it. If it helps, count. One on the inhalation, two on the exhalation. Three on the inhalation, four on the exhalation. When you get to ten, start over.

That's it. Your brain will jump all over the place. You'll start thinking of all sorts of things—anything other than the breathe. This is often called the "monkey mind," and you can't fight it. Instead, whenever you notice your mind is thinking about something other than the breath counting, just gently note it and return your attention to the breath.

At the end of your session, take a moment to notice how you feel, both mentally and physically. If you give this a shot for just a couple of days, I think you'll be surprised at the results you get back. Very quickly, the mind starts to retrain itself to behave in a less scattered, less frenetic way, and this new sense of focus and clarity can have a profound impact on every area of life.

Attack: Your Personal Mission Statement

You're familiar with corporate mission statements, but you may have less experience with *personal* mission statements—sometimes called purpose statements. Steven R. Covey kicked the practice off in his motivational classic *The 7 Habits of Highly Successful People*, and the practice has grown since then. Personal mission statements are useful for two reasons.

First, there's something to be gained from sitting back and reflecting upon how you see yourself and your purpose in the world. As we've just discussed in the previous section, people's heads go a mile a minute, and it's all too easy to get caught up in the turmoil of the world without ever taking some time out for introspection.

Secondly, a personal mission statement gives us a greater sense of focus and a cause to rally behind. Whenever things get hectic, you can return to your attention to your personal statement to remind yourself who you are and what you're about. This will become even more important once you start finding success. When your life starts changing, it's easy to suddenly look back and find that you and what you stand for have also changed. Your personal statement can help you avoid that fate.

Author William Arruda suggests a three-part template for how to write these, which you can use if you find it helpful: The value you create + who you're creating it for + the expected outcome.[6] For example: I use my expertise in commerce to bring products to people to help them live better lives while spending less money.

Here are a couple of good ones from highly successful CEOs, some of whom you probably know:

"To have fun in my journey through life and learn from my mistakes."
– Sir Richard Branson, founder of the Virgin Group

"To be a teacher. And to be known for inspiring my students to be more than they thought they could be."
– Oprah Winfrey, founder of OWN, The Oprah Winfrey Network

"To use my gifts of intelligence, charisma, and serial optimism to cultivate the self-worth and net-worth of women around the world."
– Amanda Steinberg, founder of DailyWorth.com

"I want to make it so that every person in the world can afford to start their own business."

---

6. Arruda, William, and Deb Dib. *Ditch. Dare. Do!: 3D Personal Branding for Executive Success: 66 Ways to Become Influential, Indispensable, and Incredibly Happy at Work!* TradesMark Press International, 2013.

– John Rampton, founder of web-hosting company Hostt.com[7]

It's your turn. Take a few minutes to reflect upon what you bring to the table, what you care about most, who you want to serve, and where you want to go in life. Then, write your first personal mission statement. You may write several over the course of the next few days or months or years, but when you find one that feels right, stick with it until it doesn't feel right anymore. (Don't be afraid to let this evolve as you and your life evolve, but only change it when it stops feeling useful.) For today, let's start with one.

_____

_____

_____

_____

_____

_____

_____

_____

Once you're set on a personal mission statement, train yourself to remind yourself each day. Let it become a mantra. You'll find that a greater sense of focus rises to the surface, and you'll have a better idea of what to say *yes* to, because those things will align with your mission.

---

7. Hendricks, Drew. "Personal Mission Statement of 13 CEOs and Lessons You Need to Learn." *Forbes.* https://www.forbes.com/sites/drewhendricks/2014/11/10/personal-mission-statement-of-14-ceos-and-lessons-you-need-to-learn/#61af584d1e5e.

Chapter Five:

Identifying Your Non-Negotiables

LET ME TELL YOU ABOUT three people I know. I've changed their names and some specifics to protect their privacy.

Dylan

Dylan was a Vice President at an enormous, thriving multi-national corporation that you have probably heard of. He had worked at this company, starting from the very bottom, for twenty years when he realized he was not happy. He had money and power to spare, but he was constantly traveling, working long hours, and struggling to facilitate change within the bureaucracy of the company. So, he quit. In his 40s, he left the company to join a scrappy, small start-up company in the same industry, taking a position that required no travel and easier hours, allowing him to spend more time with his family and pursue other non-work interests, something he hadn't really done in decades.

Janice

Janice finished law school at a young age and immediately began practicing law. She was an excellent lawyer; her natural charisma and strong demeanor translated well to making confident, intelligence arguments in court, and her clients appreciated her for her good nature and attentiveness. After a few years, however, Janice found the work demoralizing. She came to realize that her job was in large part to argue professionally, and she didn't like the way that made her feel, even if it was for a good reason. It was taking an emotional and psychological toll. What's more, she was inundated constantly by the worst parts of society, surrounded by stories of crime, infidelity, and corporate malfeasance. She decided it wasn't a good fit, and she walked away. She went back to school to study writing. Now she focuses her energy on publishing poems, and she works as an editor.

Michael

Michael went to college for software engineering and snagged a good gig early on as a software developer at a start-up. The start-up grew rapidly, and his role grew along with it. Within a few years, he'd worked his way up to a senior developer position, managing a team of programmers. There was a lot to like. The money was great, and he had significant creative control over the projects they worked on. After a couple years, however, he was sick of it. He was sick of cubicles and board rooms. He was tired of staring at a computer screen and bored of looking at code. He too walked away, returning to the job he'd had in college, a job he loved—waiting tables at an Italian restaurant. He loved the people he'd worked with there, the money was enough to support his frugal lifestyle, and at night he focused on writing a sports blog and devoting time to relationships.

The Point

We've talked a lot about the kind of scenario where someone isn't happy with their level of success and starts making changes, even later in life, to transform their situation. In these three examples, these people made radical professional changes that resulted in way happier lives but far less income— because for them, the financial independence isn't what they valued most. And they're awesome because they show how the core principles we're thinking about work in so many different situations. It's not hard to imagine Janice being afraid to walk away from a law practice to write poetry, and most people wouldn't have the guts to make that leap. It's easy to see how Dylan could have scoffed at the risk involved with leaving a very financially comfortable position to join up with a smaller, family-owned company. Even though Michael was perfectly happy waiting tables a couple of days a week and made enough money to be satisfied, you can imagine how some people might scoff at that choice. But all three of these people took a step back to reflect honestly about their lives, made a plan of action, and put it into play. In other words, they breathed, focused, and attacked. That's what we're all about.

All three of these people identified their non-negotiables, but it took each of them decades to do it. Each of them was in their early 40s when they made these career switches.

Many people would happily switch places with all three of these people, which just goes to show you how different people's priorities really are. Because something's a "good job" or someone's "marriage material" on the surface doesn't mean it's right *for you*. Which brings us to my next point.

Knowing What You Really Want

There's no secret technique to knowing what you really want. You already know. The problem is that sometimes that knowledge lies deep down within us, and it can be difficult to differentiate what we our must-haves _really_ are from what we only *think* they are. Most of us will gain some clarity simply through the process of living. There's trial and error, for one. (Who hasn't gotten something they wanted, only to realize it wasn't what they thought it was?) There's also the heightened self-awareness that comes from growing as a person, both through the intentional process of self-improvement (including a lot of the work we'll do later in this book) as well as just growing older and wiser.

That said, you can get to the truth more quickly if you do some soul-searching and try to identify what some call "compensatory reactions." Way back in the beginning of this book, I talked about how many—if not most—people just kind of arbitrarily drift through life, making decisions without an overarching long term plan, usually informed by their emotional response to changes. Our personal history can play an overbearing role in how we progress, and we may not even realize it.

In the previous case of Dylan, for instance? He got married young and had a child immediately. Money was a constant source of anxiety. He and his wife lived in a tiny trailer initially, a place without running water or climate control—on winter nights, they ran the stove with its door open to heat the trailer. It's easy to understand how he could lie in bed beside his new wife and son, look around at his surroundings, and feel a deep need to make a change. Once he secured a job with an opportunity for upward mobility, he never looked back. He worked his ass off, flying upwards through the ranks, determined to make sure his family was always comfortable and secure. What's more, making enough to live comfortably in the present wasn't enough: he wanted to become successful enough that they never had to worry about anything again. And that's what he did. So that model of action became the habit, and this became the course he set himself upon, and it wasn't until 20 years later that he stopped to ask himself the hard questions. He *thought* a huge salary was a non-negotiable, but the *real* non-negotiable was spending enough time with his family.

It's easy to get wrapped up in the mindset of "if I can just do [insert thing], everything will be okay." We're born hungry, hungry for a dozen different things—security, prosperity, and intimacy are a few. True contentment isn't something produced by changing your external situation, though. It's a state of mind. That doesn't mean you shouldn't strive for the things you want, but you'll be happiest in the long run when you know yourself well enough to know that your goals are set for the right reasons.

Thoughts on Minimalism

Minimalism as an idea has its roots in art and design, but it has also gained steam as a lifestyle movement, and it ties in closely with identifying your non-negotiables. Minimalists strive for simpler, freer lives by pretty much only sticking to their non-negotiables in terms of what they own and how they spend their time. Part of this is about being more discerning with the things you own, but at its heart what it's really all about is taking "saying no" to the next level.

In *Fight Club*, Tyler Durden's attitudes towards society and consumerism became a kind of siren call for legions of college-aged guys just taking their first steps into the world of free thinking. In the movie, Durden blows up his own apartment full of nice things to free himself from the pressure of having to care about them. "The things you own," he remarks, "end up owning you." Or to put a harder edge on it: "You are not your f*cking khakis." Looking back, *Fight Club*'s attempts at being philosophical are at times childish, but I can get behind the broad sentiment here. Notorious B.I.G. also knew this: more money can lead to more problems.

The minimalist philosophy asks you to eliminate things from your life that you can live without. In addition to possessions, this also includes ways you spend your time and energy. Anything that *consumes resources* (time, money, energy.) Basically, implementing some minimalist strategies in your life helps you identify your non-negotiables through process of elimination.

Many minimalists suggest buying quality goods if it's economically feasible, for example. Good clothes that are still financially reasonable may last much longer than more cheaply made clothes.

You'd be surprised at what you can live without. Do you pay for cable because you always have, but nowadays find yourself watching nothing but Netflix? You might save yourself a couple of hundred dollars a year by ditching it. If you find a few places in your life like that, places where you splurge unnecessarily, you can free up significant resources.

Another example: when financial experts help people re-evaluate their budgets, cars are often one of the first things to come under the gun. At its core, a car's purpose is to get you safely from one location to another. Everything else is icing on the cake. A new and expensive car might stick you with a payment of hundreds of dollars a month for years when you may be able to easily buy a car for much, much less that's not sexy but gets the job done and doesn't require you to make monthly payments. That frees up that cash to be used in support of something non-negotiable. Or, better yet, perhaps you find out that you can actually make do just fine with a bike. Writer Colin Wright notes that one of his non-negotiables is a fast, high-performing laptop. He lives a nomadic lifestyle and works digitally, so it makes perfect sense. He never has to worry about putting funds into those laptops, because he's not spending the money on other expensive things that he used to think he needed but now knows he really doesn't (like an iPhone.)[13]

In terms of how your time is spent, you may take a critical look at your schedule and realize that you're committed to all sorts of things that you could do without. Ridding yourself of unnecessary obligations and just keeping things simple results in a much freer life and much more free time to re-devote however you'd like.

Professional Non-Negotiables

Many of you will find yourselves in leadership roles at companies, whether they're yours or someone else's. Defining some non-negotiables for your entire organization go a long ways towards creating a company culture. Consider these two dueling examples. The first: "Never take your work home with you." This would encourage employees to concentrate on a healthy work/life balance and communicates to them that there are things in life in addition to work that are important and need time and attention. On the other hand, how about this second one? "Always do what it takes to get the job done, no matter what." A company where that's a known non-negotiable might stress

13. Wright, Colin. "Minimalism Explained." https://exilelifestyle.com/minimalism-explained.

performance above all else in a fast-paced or high-pressure environment. The right kind of culture to foster will depend on entirely on the nature of each individual business, but the take-away here is that *you should take steps to create the culture you want to exist in your workplace.*

These non-negotiables may also govern the ways employees interact with each other—demanding honesty or prohibiting gossiping, for example.

You should also consider non-negotiables in new hires. Again, what's right depends entirely on your specific situation, but below are a few qualities that will never let you down as you grow your company:

Adaptability

Particularly in a start-up environment, the ability to adopt to new situations, projects, technologies, etc. is invaluable. Adaptability also demonstrates

Being Teachable

Few employees will be perfect the minute they walk through the door. Even if they're highly qualified, doing the work at your specific company is its own animal, and it takes time and experience to become fully developed in a new role. Employees who can't be taught become liabilities in the long run. We've all known people like this, right? When they're coached, they either become defensive and take suggestions as personal attacks, or perhaps they seem to take the lesson to heart but it never seems to result in real change. Employees like these are best avoided.

Ability to Communicate

Good employees can communicate well, both face-to-face and in writing. Being unable to write clearly and professionally reflects poorly on your company, but it can also easily result in misinterpretation of crucial information.

Drive

What drives everyone is different, and part of your job as a leader is figuring out what drives each of your employees. However, you're ideally looking for employees who have an innate desire to achieve things. These are the employees who actively strive to further your mission and to become better at their jobs as opposed to just punching a card and collecting a check.

Empathy

Employees with empathy are easier to manage and work better in teams. Work life can be stressful, and sometimes it's easy to forget that co-workers, bosses, and customers are all people, and that they're all just trying to do their jobs and get through the week as best they can. Empathetic employees go about their work with the idea in mind that their performance has real effects on the lives of others.

Relationship Non-Negotiables

If you're relatively early in your dating career, it's probably going to take some experience to figure out your non-negotiables. It's good to have an idea of what you're looking for, but most people in healthy long-term relationships have had a few terrible ones under their belt. Relationships are both terribly hard and terribly educational.

And what do you do when your partner either wants something different, or has characteristics you've deemed incompatible? Well, if these are truly non-negotiable for you, they have to be willing to make a change. If they're unwilling or incapable, the relationship's headed for disaster, and you'd probably be best off planning an exit strategy that leaves everyone on good terms. The opposite is also true: if you think something's non-negotiable for your *partner* but it's something you can't give them, you should talk to them. Nothing about this process is meant to cause unhappiness. Rather, what it's all about is recognizing the reality of who you are and what you need and then not being afraid to act accordingly. You don't do anyone any favors when you prolong a relationship that's ultimately going to leave both parties unhappy. Don't waste each other's time.

Breathe: Clean Out Your Closet

This one's got some action attached to the reflection. It's time to clean out your closets, both figuratively and literally. Getting rid of old clothes is one of the easiest little corners of life to declutter. You might even start by setting aside the clothes you're definitely going to keep. (Your non-negotiable wardrobe items!) With stuff you're on the fence about, ask yourself the following questions:

- Does it even fit?

- Does it actually look good on me?

- Have I worn it in the last six months?

- Will I wear it in the next six months?

If you can't answer "yes" to at least three—preferably four—of these questions, it's safe to donate. If the thought of doing this makes you nervous, shoot for one bag of old clothes at first. Donate them to a thrift store, and check in with yourself a week later. I'll bet you any amount of money you won't be missing the items you donated.

Often we hang on to stuff we used to love that doesn't really have a place in our life anymore (see a metaphor there?), or things we have some sentimental attachment to. I also keep some things for sentimental value— but not a million. How often do you take these objects out and quietly smile at them, fondly reminiscing? Probably not often. Sometimes people keep things around not because it truly makes them happier to do it, but because they think it will feel bad to say goodbye. But they're just *things*. Your memories are not attached to them. You will not forget just because the things are gone. In many cases, those things can go on to live second lives in someone else's wardrobe, which is a beautiful thing. Instead of gathering dust in your closet, the item will be making someone happy.

While you're doing this, think about what you're unwilling to part with—the things in your life that you have to protect at all costs—and the things that, like old clothes, you can leave behind.

Focus: A Friendly Reminder

If your non-negotiables are things you have yet to achieve, you'll achieve them most quickly when you apply laser-like focus to the effort. And since you'll already have decided that other pursuits are things you don't necessary need, you'll know it will be okay to divert some of that time, money, and energy into making those non-negotiables a reality. Once you're set up in such a way that you've got your non-negotiables covered, you can turn your attention back to other, less pressing things.

Attack: Your Non-Negotiables

It's time to write some down. It's not enough to just think about it for a few minutes. Taking the time to put ink to paper, making it concrete, also makes the ideas concrete in your mind. There's power to physically writing your non-negotiables down, and it might be interesting to return to them months or years from now to see how well you kept them. You can choose the non-negotiables in your everyday life, in your professional life, your romantic life, or all of the above.

Chapter Six:

Minimum Viable Product (MVP)

LET'S SAY YOUR KID COMES up to you and proudly announces they want to make a lemonade stand. *Awesome,* you think. *I'm going to encourage this entreprenuerial spirit.* Let's pretend his name is Ralph. You buy a car-load of lemons for Ralph. You're not just doing Plain Jane yellow lemonade, though—hell no, not for *your* kid. You buy some other fruit to do infusions, and you're definitely going to offer pink lemonade. You're getting excited now, positive you're setting little Ralph up for success. You have a cute little uniform made, maybe even business cards. You name the business "Ralph's Craft Lemonade" and have a friend mock up a logo concept. You sink a few hundred bucks into lumber and and construct the sharpest-looking lemonade stand anyone's ever seen. At last, everything's done, and you pat Ralph on the back and say, *Go get 'em, Tiger.*

Ralph's meteoric rise to success doesn't happen. A day later, he's over it. He hasn't sold any lemonade at all, and standing in the heat is getting old. Instead of pressing forward until his business turns a profit, he goes inside and enjoys air conditioning and Nintendo.

Well, you blew it. You screwed up your kid's summer and drained your wallet, and for what? Ralph didn't need all of that. What he needed was a pitcher of lemonade and maybe a wagon. If he'd dipped his toe in the water and tested both his product and the market, he might've learned that nobody in the neighborhood even likes lemonade and that some other beverage would've been the wiser choice. Or he might've learned that people were interested in buying his lemonade but that offering all those varieties meant he had to charge a dollar for a glass of lemonade and that nobody would pay more than 50 cents. You could've taught Ralph a good lesson about market analysis, but instead you taught him that hard work doesn't pay off.

Ralph needed an MVP—a Minimum Viable Product. In the simplest terms, a Minimum Viable Product is exactly what it sounds like: a product with just enough features to be marketable to your first customers. Entering the playing field with an MVP lets you iterate and improve upon your product based on feedback from customers, experimentation, and data collection. You're investing only the minimum amount of time and money on a product in its infancy, which minimizes risk and also has the handy byproduct of giving you working capital to further develop the product, should it prove successful. The term rose to prominence in the early 2000s, especially through the work of Eric Ries, who championed the approach in his highly influential book *The Lean Startup*.

Not all products are going to be winners, and an MVP helps you avoid pouring too many resources into a flop. Most entrepreneurs leave a string of discarded ideas and unpopular products in their wake, and that's part of the process. We discussed that way back in Chapter 1—most people's best ideas aren't their first ideas. For most, hitting the big time will be a process that will involve trial and error, growth through experience, and lessons learned the hard way. Throwing everything behind an unproven idea is a bit like putting all of one's proverbial eggs in the same basket: if it's not a booming success, you're doomed.

The MVP is the "first step" of the business world, and remember: most people never find the conviction to take that first step.

Perhaps the most famous early example of a major company utilizing an MVP is Dropbox. If you don't know, Dropbox is a service for syncing and transferring files, even very large ones. As you can imagine, developing Dropbox was no small feat. Imagine if they'd churned out a fast, always-on network with proper security and functionality right out of the gate, only to find that nobody was interested in using it or found it too confusing—they would've sunk before they started.

There was *risk* associated with the *assumption* that there was a market for Dropbox, because no other product like it existed. So, Dropbox's developers tested the market. Rather than actually doing any coding at all, they produced an explainer video demonstrating how the proposed site would work and how people would interact with it, then spread the video. The response was positive, and the team knew they probably had a hit on their hands, so they charged forward. The rest is history.

Pivoting

Creating your MVP and collecting information through customer responses is only part of the equation. If the response is good, then you're gold. But what if you learn that your initial assumptions about what would work prove faulty? That's when it's time to *pivot*. Usually, when people talk about pivoting, they're talking about making changes to your product or service, but technically any segment of a business model can change: it might include costs, customer acquisition strategy, supply chain partners, etc. For our purposes, we're focusing on pivoting in terms of the core idea of a business.

Pivoting is all about staying limber and adapting to the market, and many ultra-successful companies have known when to do it. Ever been to a Starbucks? The hyper-ubiquitous coffee chain started as a supplier of espresso makers. They'd been in business a full 12 years before they ever tried opening an actual coffee shop and brewing for customers. When that showed signs of being more lucrative than selling machines, they essentially scrapped the first model altogether and poured all of their effort into opening new cafes.

One of my favorites is the photo-sharing website Flickr. Flickr actually started as an online game called Game Neverending, in which players could interact with each other by buying and selling items, traveling the world, chatting, etc. Players also had the ability to upload and share their photos with each other, which proved really popular. Game Neverending's owners decided to go all-in on photo sharing, rebranded to Flickr, and became a success story.

And speaking of video games, Nintendo tried all sorts of business ideas before they settled on making games. The company had previous lives as a producer of instant rice, a taxi service, a hotel chain, and a vacuum cleaner manufacturer, among others.

When you put an MVP out into the world, listen to what the world tells you. People will tell you what they want, even if they themselves don't know it yet. Once you learn to hear them, nothing can stop you.

MVPs for Health

This book isn't just about business, and you can extend the logic of MVPs into other pursuits with a little imagination.

There's an endlessly quoted statistic floating free out there, a depressing assertion that 95% of people who attempt diets fail. The typical follow-up is that many succeed in losing some weight during the first six months or so of implementing a diet program, but that virtually all gain it back—and then some—within at least a couple of years. Too many people read this and think, *I hear you loud and clear: it's obviously not worth trying.* So, they don't, and in choosing not to they too relegate themselves to the 95% who don't take that first step.

Here's the thing, though. For one, that statistic is not based on much of anything. It has become medical lore, and nobody's entirely sure where it came from. The best hypothesis comes from Dr. Kelly D. Brownell at Yale's Center for Eating and Weight Disorders, who believes that the statistic first appeared in a 1959 study of only 100 people, and that the claim spread like wildfire from there.[8] So, it all boiled down to one little study with one tiny sample size, and dozens of other studies since then have taken issue with it.

---

8. "95% Regain Lost Weight. Or Do they?" *The New York Times.* https://www.nytimes.com/1999/05/25/health/95-regain-lost-weight-or-do-they.html

Regardless, this pessimistic contention about the lasting effects of dietary changes nudges people towards inaction. People figure that only a few bright and shining few, the special successful outliers, will be the ones who maintain a healthy change in their routine. And perhaps that familiar voice in the back of their heads already tells them: *you're not special.*

Half of the equation of people's failure to stick to healthier eating routines might be their assumption that they'll fail—which becomes a self-fulfilling prophecy—but the other half is a lack of good data. A longterm plan for better health involves significant lifestyle changes *that can be maintained over time*. You have to be able to live with the changes you make. You have to find ways to live a healthier lifestyle that enrich your life, not ones that you instinctively view as suffering and sacrificing. Being healthier should make your life better, not worse. You should *feel* better. People do it wrong, so they fail in the long run. You probably know people like this, who usually talk about changes in diet routines as temporary programs. "I'm doing keto," they'll say, or "I'm on the South Beach diet." Or whatever. The very language of it suggests a temporary strategy that they're employing. The minute they've reached whatever their goal is, they revert to their normal routine, and so they also return to their normal results.

This is where the magic of the MVP comes into play. For those of us that aren't perhaps naturally inclined towards healthy habits, the MVP keeps us from failing outright by allowing us to lose battles without ceding the war.

An example: Ralph's an adult now, and his New Year's Resolution is to hit the gym at least three days a week and to not buy takeout on weeknights. He hopes this will improve his general health and level of fitness, as well as saving him some money by cooking at home. He signs up for a gym membership at the fancy new gym in town and loads up on groceries.

For the first few days, he's pumped. It feels good to be making good changes. He doesn't have time to hit the gym in the evening, especially if he's cooking, so he wakes up an hour early and goes before work. He imagines a version of himself that's fitter, strong, faster, generally more alert and vital.

Barely a week in, things begin to change. The gym he'd signed up for had attracted him with its new facilities and flashy marketing, but going in the morning means he's hitting horrible morning traffic. To get to work on time, he'll have to start getting up even earlier, or perhaps going at night. And the waking up earlier becomes its own problem: he's really hating it, and he feels exhausted all day. By the time he gets home, the last thing he wants to do is cook. He's starting to dread dinner. Within a couple of weeks, Frank is miserable and he's done. He starts slipping. He drops those gym days from 3 to 2. He gets fast food on the way home from work a couple of times. By the end of the month, he has abandoned his plan altogether.

Since Frank shot for the moon, his failure stings all the more. Whether he realizes it or not, part of his brain has an idea of what healthy routines should look like, and that same part of his brain has also now learned that he can't maintain them.

What if he'd implemented a Minimum Viable Health Plan? His problem was that his strategies were not sustainable for *him* and *his* lifestyle. What if he'd taken it a step at a time to see what worked, and then let his strategy evolve from there? Perhaps in the MVP version of his health strategy, instead of the gym membership he tries biking to work one day a week? If that turns out to not be sustainable, no sweat: he can try something else without feeling like he's failed completely. But what if he really likes it? What if he feels awake and energized the rest of the work day? Before you know it, Frank could be riding a bike to work 5 days a week, and he might even love it. Just like that, a part of his life has evolved in a healthy way that makes him happier—not a way that makes him feel like he's putting himself through an ordeal.

Maybe he tries cooking for a week, but he realizes it's taking too long, he doesn't like the outcome, and he's not really saving as much money as he thought he would. Well, the MVP methodology tells him he should pivot—he should just not worry about the cooking and try something else. So instead he looks for takeout options that are healthier than the places he ordered out from before. He finds a few places he enjoys, and he starts subbing out those healthy options for the unhealthy ones that were his habit before.

MVPs for Creative Projects

There's a particular kind of creator who never finishes projects. I come across them all the time, especially among aspiring authors. They've been working on a book for years, rewriting and revising endlessly, perhaps even romanticizing the effort. Many famous authors were compulsive reworkers, after all: you'll recall from before that Mark Twain spent a decade on *Adventures of Huckleberry Finn*. The difference is that, ultimately, guys like Mark Twain knew when to let the baby bird out of the nest, to let the work out into the world to either fly or crash.

Musicians are not immune. Think Guns and Roses, who famously announced a studio album called *Chinese Democracy* in the 90s but allowed it to languish in "development Hell" for years, until it became a running joke. By 2000, it was the most expensive album of all time, with the band having racked up $18 million in expenditures by re-recording over and over again, firing personnel, etc. The pressure must've been enormous. After sinking that much time and money into an album and spending years and years hyping its eventual release, it would pretty much need to be the best album ever to live up expectations, right? It didn't drop until 2008, about 20 years after its initial announcement, and the reception was good, but it was not enough to catapult the band into a new era to compete with their earlier work.

There's something comforting about having a project, and there's a sense of safety that comes with keeping it private. If you never push the work out into the world, you can never fail. But taking that step, despite how scary it might be, makes all the difference.

Breathe: Assumptions are Made to be Wrong

When you have an idea for a project or a goal, assumptions come with the territory. Often, they'll be wrong. They won't be wrong because you're stupid or because your thinking is wrong—they'll be wrong because you don't have all the data yet. Testing your assumptions and recognizing when they need adjusting is how you get that data. So don't be overly precious or sensitive about your ideas. Often, the *real* genius idea is somewhere within the idea as you see it in its infancy. Don't be worried if your ideas aren't immediately taking off. And don't be worried if you have big ideas but few resources to implement them—just think of an MVP you can reach with the resources you do have.

Focus: Reign in Those Ideas

There are people who move through life in an average way, and there are people with the capacity for real greatness who never quite launch. For the latter, often the problem is a wealth of ideas and a lack of focus, time, or energy. If you find yourself involved in dozens of ventures at once, you'll never finish any of them. Likewise, if you're focused on dozens of ideas pertaining to one project in particular, you'll be developing that project forever. Instead, try to think about what steps you need to take to move your project to an MVP state. All the inspiration in the world won't do you any good unless you learn to hone that inspiration and transform it into practical action.

Attack: Create a Roadmap

Good business plans have detailed plans of action spread out over months or years—activities to do and goals to meet for Quarter 1, Quarter 2, etc. For your purposes that form of organization may be an awkward fit, but regardless you'll benefit from thinking of progress in terms of phases and steps. Whatever your current Big Goal is, let's break it down.

Phase One: Prework

Your Phase One goal is to set up the tools you need before you can actually start implementing your MVP. That includes assembling a team, if any, any initial materials or data needed, etc. It's your pre-work. Don't get bogged down here.

Phase One Action Steps:

1. _____
   _____

2. _____
   _____

3. _____
   _____

4. _____
   _____

Phase Two: The MVP

What do you need to get to the MVP? If you're selling a physical product, for example, that might just be a prototype, or even mock-ups of the product. It may be a minimally functional version of a website or service. Either way, boil it down to the minimum number of steps needed to get your idea into the world in a way where others can interact with it.

Phase Two Action Steps:

1. _____
   _____

2. _____
   _____

3. _____
   _____

4. _____
   _____

Phase 3: Acting on Feedback

You can't know ahead of time what the specifics here will be, but plan on implementing initial changes early based on what kind of response you get from your MVP. For example, let's imagine you're selling clothing online via an e-commerce website, and in your first week everyone buy's Women's Clothing but nobody buys Men's Clothing. In that case, perhaps you'd want to just focus on the Women's market going forward. So an example action step ahead of time might be something like, "Remove products expected to underperform" or "Expand product line in relation to top sellers during opening week."

Phase Three Action Steps:

1. _____
   _____
2. _____
   _____
3. _____
   _____
4. _____
   _____

Beyond these three phases, it's all up to you. But always plan on having a roadmap ahead of you—this will keep you on task and keep you honest. You'll know when you're failing to knock items off of your checklist or when you're performing ahead of schedule. Always have a plan!

Chapter Seven:

Radical Candor

"Radical Candor" is a bunch of things. It's a management philosophy, most importantly. But it's also a brand, a company, a book[9], and a podcast, all of which support and promote the ideas of Radical Candor. At this point, it's something of a movement, and the woman at the forefront is its creator, Kim Scott. Scott's resume is nothing to scoff at. She was a manager at Google, then made faculty at Apple University. She's been a CEO coach for Twitter and Dropbox. The reason she's highly sought after by many of the world's most successful companies is that her methods work, and successful people love things that are successful.

Scott strives to create "bullshit-free zones" in which feedback is constantly given and received, but in a way in which all team members feel supported and empowered. She puts horrible bosses in the crosshairs. And some of the horrible bosses she most reviles are the nice ones.

Why do *you* need to know about Radical Candor? For one, because a lot of you are reading this with business progression in mind. But even for those of you who don't see managing teams in your future, Radical Candor's lessons about successful and direct communication translate across all areas

---

9. Scott, K. M. (2017). *Radical candor: How to be a kickass boss without losing your humanity*. New York: St. Martin's Press.

of life, assuming you interact with other human beings. The most important summation of the Radical Candor philosophy is this: Care Personally, Criticize Directly. Remember that phrase. Make it a mantra.

Care Personally, Criticize Directly

The best thing you can do for your employees is help them be successful. There's no real debate to be had about this—time and time again, studies reinforce the idea that people value fairness and effectiveness over niceness. Incidentally, this is also true in academic settings. Students rate professors higher who they feel are *fair*, not necessarily ones who they think are *nice*. The reason for this is simple: in these roles, you are not there to be the other person's friend. In an employer-employee relationship, for example, you're both there to get a job done. That's the reason you go to work in the morning. You've got work to do, and you receive some form of compensation for that work. That doesn't mean you can't be friends, and if you can, that's some nice icing on the cake. But you need to be a boss first, and you need to help them succeed. If they fail and you haven't tried to stop it, that's on you. Scott describes a situation where a member of her team at Google was universally liked and respected, but he was basically terrible at his job. His name was Bob. She tried to steer him in the right direction through vaguely praising him when he did things well, but of course that didn't result in any performance changes. We've probably all had Bobs in our lives, great people who didn't do great work. Eventually, other members of the team were becoming increasingly agitated at the way Bob's incompetence was affecting their own work. Scott invited Bob out for coffee, and then she fired him. The first words out of his mouth? "Why didn't you *tell* me?" Then, a moment later: "Why didn't *anyone* tell me? I thought you all cared about me!"

She'd failed him. In fact, the whole team had failed him. All along, Bob had no way of knowing he wasn't pulling his weight, so he didn't change. Why would he? Instead, he got blindsided by losing his job. In Radical Candor terminology, this is referred to as "ruinous empathy." When you care so much about hurting someone's feelings that you fail to tell them what they need to hear, that's ruinous empathy. That's not being a good boss *or* a good friend.

Instead, the Radical Candor way is to provide truthful, direct feedback, and to provide it often. Sometimes it's going to hurt. (This is sometimes playfully called "front-stabbing.") But feedback doesn't have to be negative! Good managers (and employees, for that matter!) should give positive feedback even more than negative. *Positive feedback tells people what you value.* It's only effective if it's *specific.* "You're doing a great job lately" is useless and serves only to make someone feel nice. It's a pat on the head. "It was really helpful how you used visual aids to help make your pitch to the client" is much more specific and gives the employee actionable information, something they can do more often. Likewise, being specific with negative feedback takes the edge off of it. Imagine telling a graphic designer, "this design could use a different color scheme—something brighter" as opposed to "this work isn't very good." The former offers some direction, while the latter feels like an indictment of the designer's judgment.

While Kim Scott was at Google, she often brought her Golden Retriever puppy, Belvedere, to work. Belvedere was loveable but not well-trained, well known for being sweet but a little spoiled. One day, when Kim was walking Belvedere, the pair stopped at a red light. Instead of sitting, the dog suddenly leapt into the road, right in the front of an oncoming taxi. Kim yanked the leash back, and Belvedere narrowly escaped being hit. A passerby approached Kim and said, "I can tell that you really love that dog," but then added, "But if you don't teach her to sit, you're going to get her killed." Then he looked at Belvedere and in a deep, forceful tone, said "SIT!" The dog sat. The man said, "See? It's not mean, it's clear."[10] Scott's ruinous empathy towards Belvedere— her love so strong she just couldn't say no to her—wasn't doing her any favors. Instead, what Belvedere really need was clear, strong education in addition to care and support.

10. "Radical Candor With Strangers." https://www.radicalcandor.com/blog/radical-candor-with-strangers/

Another important note: feedback is always more useful in the moment. Right after something happens, pulling an employee aside for a brief moment of feedback will always work better than saving up that feedback for a later date. That's how a shocking number of companies do things, especially large corporations that are clumsily trying to implement feedback systems but leaving out the human dynamic. The employee will sit down with the boss a few times a year, and the boss will recite a laundry list of pros and cons about the employee's performance, and it can all feel very overwhelming and unpleasant. Creating a culture of frequent and casual feedback fosters an openness and a sense of striving for communal goals.

How to Give a Damn

Most importantly, when everyone on the team knows they're cared about and knows that everything's in service of your larger goals, that feedback doesn't feel personal. It's not the employer attacking the employee—it's both of you attacking the problem.

These ideas apply to all social interactions, not just workplace communication. Think back to our discussion of friendships and toxicity. When you sincerely care about others, they'll be less likely to get defensive when you approach them with concerns about your relationship. Or, on the other hand, if you never give positive feedback to your friends and loved ones, they'll never know the extent to which you care. Remember, positive feedback tells others what you value.

So in the workplace, how do you show you care? We've already mentioned one way, which is to always try to set them up for success. Another is to *ask for* teammates' feedback, whether you're an employee or an employer. Really listen to it. This demonstrates that you value their opinions and expertise.

Another strong way to demonstrate that you personally care is to try to understand your teammates' long-term goals for themselves and their lives. You may find that the reasons they're in their role aren't the ones you'd assume, and you may be able to support their goals in a mutually beneficial way. If you can do that, your team members will work harder and happier. Everyone wins.

Don't Schmooze

The biggest thing "caring directly" *isn't* is schmoozing. Don't kiss ass, make fake smalltalk, or pay lip service to teammates' personal lives in ways that feel false. Whatever you do, don't take center stage in organizing frequent after-work social outings.

I've got an acquaintance who's in a managerial position. I'll keep it vague so as not to out her, but her company requires her to hold a weekly review meeting with her team. So, in an attempt to be nice, cool, and caring, she holds those meetings after work at a nearby bar. Unbeknownst to her, her employees *hate it*. It essentially extends their work day. They have their own lives, friends, and loved ones outside of work, and these weekly bar meetings take time away from that. What's more, since she's the boss, her employees don't feel comfortable saying no. In essence, she's just ensuring they're working part of their Wednesday nights in addition to their normal work hours. Don't be that kind of boss.

How to Receive Feedback

If you buy into Kim Scott's logic—which I do—then a necessary take-away is that most people who give you feedback are doing it poorly. Chances are, they're not saying what they need to be saying. They're doing some sort of mental calculus to find a line where they can communicate *enough* of what they need to get across without offending you or stepping outside of the established social norms of your shared environment. The other insidious part about this is that there can also be baggage built right into the power dynamic that adds a whole new dimension to the communication. When members of one race speak to another, or one gender to another, or any other form of difference, the fact that one person's in a position of power and the other one isn't takes on additional weight. The same acquaintance

I just mentioned, for example, the one who schmoozes with her team over beers? She has far more trouble giving feedback to the male members of her team, because she feels as though they don't take her seriously or really acknowledge that she's in a position of authority. I have no way of knowing if that's true; for all I know they may have the utmost respect for her. I don't know them. What matters is that *she feels* like this is the case, and it colors her interactions with them whenever the conversation is unpleasant.

For Radical Candor to work, all the parties involved have to know (*really* know) that no feedback is made from a position of bad faith. That means it takes two to tango. Most likely, many of you are in positions where you have a boss right now. Even if they don't subscribe to this methodology, and even if their feedback is completely unhelpful, you still gain from assuming good faith. It can help you turn their garbage feedback into something positive, and it helps you keep an optimistic and healthy mindset about the work you're doing. Feeling picked on, on the other hand, sours the entire endeavor, and you should never let anyone sabotage your work life like that, even if it's unintentional. We spend *way* too much of our waking hours at work to tolerate them being consistently awful.

Breathe: What Feedback Do You Give the World?

Spend a few minutes reflecting on the feedback you send into the world, both literally and also through your behavior and body language. How often are you ruinously empathetic, sparing someone's feelings when you'd really be helping them better by speaking directly? How often do you fail to mean what you say and say what you mean? How often do you stick up for yourself?

Think of the people in your life that you care about the most. How often do you give them feedback, and how often do you solicit theirs? That is to say, how often do you express your appreciation for them? And how often do you ask them about their own lives and *really* listen to the response?

You're a walking, talking electronic billboard, flashing away, sending messages out into the world through everything you do

Focus: Affecting Change

This "Focus" is going to be more active than others. Here's what I'd like to encourage you to do: rearrange a room in your house. You don't have to spend all day moving furniture, but switch some things up. Redecorate a little. What we're trying to do is affect change in our environment in a literal sense—moving our possessions around, changing the look of a space.

While you're doing that, picture the change you'd like to see in either your workplace or your social circle. Imagine the version of your job in which the office is a "no bullshit zone." There are plenty of things at work to worry about and plenty of ways to occupy your time, but once you decide to try to bring Radical Candor to life in your workplace, you need to prioritize it and set aside some of the lesser concerns. In other words, *focus*.

When you're done changing up a room, I think you're going to be surprised at how you feel. By now I sound like a broken record, but I'll say it again: the most important step is the first one, and most people never take it. That includes changing the environment they live in. Many people haven't ever changed things since they've moved in, but *bam!*—in just a few minutes you've transformed your situation in a small but concrete way.

Attack: For Bosses

For each of your employees, map out a plan to have three conversations. Kim Scott endorses having each of these:

- A conversation about their past.

- A conversation about their future.

- A conversation about how their current role can help them get from their past to their future.

If you have these conversations, you'll understand your employees' motivations, hopes, and goals. Aligning their work life with those goals will turbocharge their performance and job satisfaction.

So, make a plan. Do it now. Use the space below to make a checklist of the people you need to have these conversations with and some opportunities you can create (i.e. lunch on Tuesday, meeting time next Thursday) to get them rolling. Don't do it later—remember, around here we like to be proactive, because knocking these things out becomes the habit.

_____

_____

_____

_____

_____

_____

_____

_____

Attack: For Employees

It can be dangerous giving feedback to your bosses unsolicited, and it can be tricky *asking* for feedback. Do it anyways. If you're not getting the kind of information you need to be effective at your job, ask your boss what you can do to further drive the team's goals.

This second part's more important: start giving specific feedback to your co-workers. For now, just focus on calling out the positives. When they do something that helps the team, tell them right away. Acknowledge it. I'd bet serious cash that others start acknowledging each other, too. Through setting an example, you can create a culture of constant feedback, even if your boss isn't doing it. Take those first steps, and others will take them, too. And when you do that, do you know what happens? You become a leader.

Chapter Eight:

Relentless Self-Reflection

REMEMBER THE HANS CHRISTIAN ANDERSEN story, "The Emperor's New Clothes?" In this story, the titular Emperor gets naked for the entire kingdom because he's led to believe he's wearing magic clothing—though a child in the crowd isn't fooled and calls him out in public. Many people misremember the details, thinking it's only about the emperor's own stupidity and vanity, forgetting the mechanic of the clothing: the weavers who promise the Emperor his clothing tell everyone that the clothing will appear invisible only to people who are stupid or unfit for their jobs. So it's not just that the Emperor's subjects are too afraid to speak truth to power, or that the Emperor himself is an utter dumbass—it's that they're afraid everyone around them will think they're stupid, too. They assume the clothing is visible to others. The child, meanwhile, is unconcerned. She knows what she sees. When we see references to this story made in popular culture, it's almost always in reference to the Emperor's ignorance: we're talking about someone who looks stupid to everyone but doesn't realize it. In actuality, there's a whole second layer to it: that everyone believes the situation is ridiculous, but they believe that others *don't* think that way and know better than them, so there's a collective ignorance at play.

Radical Candor would've saved the Emperor from this situation, by the way. Just saying.

In your own life, you're both the Emperor and a peasant. The Emperor should have been able to take a long, honest look at himself in the mirror, see what was right in front of him, and think, *oh God, these weavers are headed to the dungeon for sure.* Instead, he chose to take the path of least mental resistance and buy into the lie that no funny business was going on. Whenever you pass on an opportunity to take an honest look at yourself, you're that guy. Congratulations. The whole kingdom's seen you naked.

Likewise, whenever you know an observation's true but are afraid to voice it because you think others will think you're dumb, you *are* being dumb. And I know that's not what you want.

A New Concept: Hansei

Every piece of this book is meant to strengthen the other pieces. They're all component parts of a whole that, hopefully, will add up to something more than the sum of its parts. That's why I wanted you to learn to become more aware of being intentional about saying "yes" and "no" to things. It's also why I wanted you to learn to sit still and meditate, even if it's only for a few minutes. It's why I wanted you to learn how to intentionally form new habits, ones that create positive changes in your life.

I've mentioned Lean business principles before. In the world of Lean and Six Sigma[11], there's a concept called *hansei* that's worth looking at. This, like many other modern business terms is borrowed from Japan. *Hansei* means "self-reflection," and it's closely tied to the Japanese notion of "kaizen"—continuous improvement. I don't want to drill down too deep into the business strategy and terminology here, but suffice it to say that *hansei* sessions are about leaders taking some time out to reflect on how they're spending their time and energy and trying to improve upon that, just as they're looking to

---

11. A set of business techniques for process improvement developed by Motorola engineer Bill Smith in 1980. Nowadays, many people subscribe to a combination of Lean and Six Sigma practices called—not very imaginatively—"Lean Six Sigma."

improve processes within the company, eliminate wasted time and money, etc. (Did you think it was a coincidence that I talked about a Japanese businessman in our first chapter? There are no coincidences here.)

This is good for everyone to do. Most of us know it at various points in our lives, though few of us make a conscious practice of it. Especially when we're younger, we're often faced with these "come to Jesus" moments, times when we're defeated or shocked or scared out of our routine and we have to step back and just ask ourselves, *"How the hell did I get here?"* When things are hard, reflection is easy. When we've got a problem, we want a solution. When we're sick, we want medicine. It's when there's not a particular ill that we let our healthy habits slip out of use, and that opens us up to failure. This is where the work of devoting just a little time for self-reflection *proactively* rather than *reactively* becomes invaluable.

An aside: This couldn't be more important when you're pushing yourself hard to succeed or just starting to hit your creative stride. It gets easy to become a workaholic, to be consumed by your ambition. In those times, things can be great, but you can lose a bit of your connection to the broader world and the larger arc of your own life story, and it's important to keep your perspective, or things can get messy.

So, Radical Candor was in large part about trying to cultivate a continual feedback loop between members of your team. And in business, *kaizen* is all about constantly taking stock of strategies and processes and making incremental improvements. The last piece of the puzzle is *you*. Radical self-reflection is about constantly taking stock of yourself, giving *yourself* feedback, and adjusting course accordingly.

Humble and Kind

In 2013, author George Saunders gave the convocation speech at Syracuse University, where he currently teaches Creative Writing. As far as writers go, Saunders is probably about as successful as you can get. In addition to enjoying his status as one of America's most revered voices, he's won countless awards, including a MacArther "Genius Grant," which comes with a nice bonus of a million dollars. Saunders spoke at length about regrets, and how he didn't regret a lot of the things he'd done in the past that others might, like working as a knuckle-puller in a slaughterhouse or swimming naked in a river in Sumatra only to realize it was full of monkey feces. After all, these experiences helped get him to where he is now. He did, however, relate one short story about something he did regret:

> In seventh grade, this new kid joined our class. In the interest of confidentiality, her Convocation Speech name will be "ELLEN." ELLEN was small, shy. She wore these blue cat's-eye glasses that, at the time, only old ladies wore. When nervous, which was pretty much always, she had a habit of taking a strand of hair into her mouth and chewing on it.

> So she came to our school and our neighborhood, and was mostly ignored, occasionally teased ("Your hair taste good?" — that sort of thing). I could see this hurt her. I still remember the way she'd look after such an insult: eyes cast down, a little gut-kicked, as if, having just been reminded of her place in things, she was trying, as much as possible, to disappear. After awhile she'd drift away, hair-strand still in her mouth. At home, I imagined, after school, her mother would say, you know: "How was your day, sweetie?" and she'd say, "Oh, fine." And her mother would say, "Making any friends?" and she'd go, "Sure, lots."

> Sometimes I'd see her hanging around alone in her front yard, as if afraid to leave it.

> And then — they moved. That was it. No tragedy, no big final hazing.

One day she was there, next day she wasn't.

End of story.[12]

Saunders went on to explain that he was basically nice to Ellen, but that more than forty years later he still felt a nagging sense of guilt. Why? Because here before him stood a human in pain, and he responded, as he described, "sensibly. Reservedly. Mildly." Saunders refers to moments like these as "failures of kindness."

For the most part, I'd argue that nobody sets out to be unkind. We know it comes from a place of smallness inside of us, something ugly and ego-driven, but we're still hard-wired to behave this way at times. Unless we train ourselves out of it, we as humans tend to forget that everyone else is as human as we are, that we're all just trying to get by, that we've all got our own bullshit to deal with. Saunders goes so far as to call our self-centeredness "Darwinian," arguing that we've evolved to think of ourselves as the center of the universe because it has afforded us an evolutionary advantage. That certainly makes sense—selflessness by definition works against our own interests, even if it's undoubtedly good for the soul.

You'll recall that Radical Candor only works if it comes from a place of kindness and humility, too. Learn to give a damn about the people you surround yourself with both in your personal life and your professional life. Those are the people that are making you successful or bringing you down. You're on this journey together.

Kindness and humility, like most true virtues, are skills. They're not something you are, they're something you do. They're habits you build, and by now you should know something about cultivating new habits. If you look at yourself honestly and critically, you'll also start recognizing the times

---

12. Saunders, George. *CONGRATULATIONS, BY THE WAY: Some Thoughts on Kindness.* Bloomsbury Publishing, 2017.

in your life that your natural inclination is to be kind and the ones when your instinct is to lash out—or, maybe even worse, to behave "sensibly, mildly" in the face of something wrong.

As you become more successful, there may be a tendency to become more egotistical, too. You will have worked to get where you are. You're doing that work right now, by reading this book and trying the things I suggest. Decide now to try to foster a greater sense of humility. Going forward, it will serve you well. The concrete benefits are never-ending: you'll stay true to your own mission, and people will naturally want to ally themselves with you.

Here's my suggestion for forming the habit of kindness. Chances are that every day, you interact with several strangers. They could be restaurant staff, other drivers on the road, or customers at businesses. Anyone, really. Start going out of your way to be kinder than you need to be at least once a day. Invite that weird co-worker out to lunch. Look a barista in the eye and smile when you get your coffee. Do something nice for your neighbor, even if they're a jerk. Especially if they're a jerk. Form the habit.

Breathe: Ignoring the Ego

Odds are good that you're not going to want to do some of the things I'm suggesting in this chapter or others. I'll repeat a fact I mentioned in an earlier chapter: the mind essentially "prefers" familiar routines and resists new things. The ego will tell you that what you're doing is working just fine, even though the higher-order parts of your mind already know it's not. If it were, you wouldn't be reading this book, would you? It's a little like eating your vegetables. When I was a kid, the idea of finishing that plate of broccoli was excruciating, something I had to be cajoled into. Now I'm an adult, and I like to eat my vegetables. I've evolved. Go figure. The point is that you should actually do these exercises, even when your mind tells you to glide over them and keep reading. Always remember: be proactive and take that first action step.

Focus: Your First Hansei Session

This isn't exactly *hansei* in the business sense, but I recommend scheduling a regular check-in with yourself. If you're trying out a brief meditation session each day as I've recommended, you might try doing this right after. Remember, attaching habits to a context helps solidify them. There's not much to it. There doesn't have to be a complex ruleset. Just reflect about what you're doing, where you want to be, and how you're going to get there. Whatever works for you is how you should proceed. Many people find that it helps them to give these *hansei* sessions some structure. You can use any set of questions that helps you, but here's a set from me:

1. Since the last session, what am I most proud of myself for? What has been my biggest success?

2. What are the biggest challenges in front of me today and for this week?

3. What steps am I going to take to overcome them?

4. Since my last session, how effective have my strategies been? What can I do to improve them?

5. How do I feel about my general behavior? Am I reacting to situations in the way I want to? If not, what can I do to correct this?

Don't worry if this feels awkward at first or if your mind wanders. What's important is to spend the minutes doing it to the best of your ability. Just like with meditation, after a few sessions, you'll start to settle into a routine, and you'll start to look forward to this little period of self-development more and more each day. You'll start to notice that your mind feels more settled and more focused, and you'll go into the rest of your day with an edge.

Attack: Try Bullet Journaling

You may have heard the term "bullet journal" in passing, or you may have even been served ads for literal bullet journals, as in specialty notebooks designed for bullet journaling. Frankly, it's too soon to tell if it's a flash-in-the-pan kind of fad, but for the time being a lot of people swear by the practice as a productivity hack.

Any journaling at all is worth trying; this is just one method. Writing things down forces you brain to organize your thoughts in a more structured and coherent way than they might live inside your head, which in turn strengthens your thought processes. For many of us, however, keeping a long-form journal wherein you write down long, rambling recollections of the day's events and your idle thoughts is perhaps too much of a pain. Bullet journaling works for people because the system allows you to write as much or as little as you need to, and it incorporates the functionality of daily planners, to-do lists, etc.

So, how do you get started? I'll walk you through each of the main functions. Grab a black notebook and a pen.

1. The Index

The Index goes at the beginning of the journal, and it's just what it sounds like: a list of the contents of the journal. Leave some blank pages at the beginning to fill it out as you go, should you pick up this habit for the long-term. You can list anything in the index you think you might need to go back to, and you just add more entries and the corresponding page ranges as you journal each day. So, for example, you might have something like this:

January — pages 1-31
    Monthly appointments — 1
    New business plan notes — 3
    Notes from leadership conference — 14
    Workout logs — 2, 8, 18, 25

…and so on. Whenever you add something that will be useful to refer back to later, you just drop a new line in the index to form a Table of Contents. Keep it casual and natural.

2. The Future Log

The Future Log just mimics the functionality of a monthly planner. Mark out spaces for each month (three months, six months, or the year), and as important dates or appointments pop up, you can jot them down in these pages. Each week, you can flip back to these pages and make sure you're not forgetting anything important.

3. Monthlies, Weeklies, and Dailies

The rest of the bullet journal system is built upon monthly, weekly, and daily sections. You might use all of these or only one—it's entirely about what works for you—but the idea is to just compartmentalize the space in the notebook accordingly and to give it some structure. Your monthly page may look like a traditional calendar, or it might not. It might include important reoccurring dates, or monthly goals, or strategies you're hoping to try out that month. Your weekly pages serve the same purpose, but at the weekly level.

Dailies are where you'll spend most of your journaling time, and here too the options are endless. The whole philosophy of bullet journaling is about customization. You might have reoccuring sections for goals, for successes that day, for how many pages you wrote or miles you ran, for what you ate, or for how much TV you watched—anything you want to track. You might have a section where you record the highlights of the day's events in a bulleted-list form. Perhaps you do a section where you leave space to write down a lesson you can take away from the day or something you want to improve upon the following day. Experiment a little and design a page based on what's important to you.

If you take this to the Internet, you'll find *tons* of example designs, tutorial videos, and articles. I recommend you do that—seeing other people's bullet journal designs will really help it all click into place.

Regardless, try this for a week. If you're seeing a pattern emerging, you're a smart one. Short, easy daily routines that help enhance productivity and focus go a long, long way towards setting you up for success. You could spend ten minutes a day on a meditation session, five on self-reflection, and five jotting down the day's bullet journal contents, and you'd only be spending 20 minutes a day giving these techniques a try.

Conclusion:

Go Forth and Conquer

I TOLD YOU THAT ATTACKING big goals is in part about becoming the kind of person who achieves those goals—that there's no prying apart the outcome you want and the person that you are. (This is in part because we largely *are* what we do.)

When you become that kind of person, the truth is that you're going to be less concerned with the actual practical outcome of your actions. If you're reading this book as a part of a run-up to starting some big new business endeavor, and that endeavor fails, ideally you'll be less concerned than you would have been before you put these ideas into practice, because you'll know that you're a better, stronger, more actualized person than when you started, and that's the truly meaningful thing here.

When you form success-building habits and skills, you have to follow through. It's like going on a crash diet, losing some weight, and then thinking you can start eating whatever again—you put the weight back on in a second. What works is finding more productive and healthier ways to live that start making you happier, not practices that you're just trying to get through on your way to some other destination.

You're reading this because you want something. And I've got bad news for you: you're never going to stop wanting things. No matter what you achieve, there will always be a next step. Tradition holds that after taking over most of the known the world, Alexander the Great wept for there were was nothing left to conquer.[14] This same sentiment has been felt generation after generation by monumentally successful people. When you think back to the happiest times in your life so far, what do you think of? People and experiences, most likely. Maybe you had less money back then. Maybe your health was better, or maybe it was worse. Maybe you were single or maybe you weren't. Chances are that whatever your life circumstances were, they didn't actually have a huge impact on how happy you were, if you think back honestly. It's not having reached the destination that really does that—it's living a good, productive, healthy life along the way. It's being the person you were born to be, the best version of yourself. Everything in this book is designed to help you take steps towards that. Strive to be the best version of yourself, and the success will follow.

What's most important is that you *take action*. It's so, so easy to do what you've always done. And it's even easier to read a book (like this one!), then put it on the shelf and move on with your day. Even if you're fired up and optimistic now, in no time your mind will be on other things. A new challenge at work will grab your attention, or maybe someone you're interested in will dominate your thoughts. When you translate your reading into action—and hopefully you've been doing that all along—*that's* when you'll start seeing real, concrete changes.

A Brief Review

Even though I've tried to keep this book short and easily digestible to make it as accessible as possible, we've covered a lot of territory. Let's take a moment to run back through the broad strokes, so you can retain the bigger picture.

---

14. While some ancient sources do record versions of this story, it has actually been proliferated in pop culture most strongly through a reference in *Die Hard*. Alexander almost certainly did not actually do this. Still, it's a good story.

Breathe, Focus, Attack

1. It's Never Too Late:

What you've done so far doesn't define what you're going to do next. You decide what you want the rest of your life to be like. What separates people who succeed from those who don't is that the former decide to *do something about it*, even if they might fail. When you do things the same way you've always done them, you'll get the same results you always have. If you're serious about changing your life, now is the time.

2. Learn to Say No:

Spend your time, energy, and money with some intentionality. Be cognizant of where your resources are going, and understand that you can only do so many things in a given day. Learn to pass gracefully on new obligations that aren't going to get you closer to the goals you really care about achieving. Don't worry, you won't hurt anyone's feelings. Don't sacrifice your hopes and dreams because you're afraid of coming across as impolite.

3. Friends:

Friends can be rocket fuel. They can help you be better, do more, and have more fun along the way. Go out of your way to make the five types of friends successful people have (mentors, partners, etc.) On the flip side, learn to recognize when relationships are toxic, and either repair them or rid yourself of them accordingly. Life's too short to be held back by them.

4. What to Say Yes To:

Find the sweet spot where you're doing something that:

- You love
- You're good at
- The world needs
- That can make money

Knock it out of the park by making a habit of forming new (good) habits and kicking the bad ones to the curb. Become the kind of person who can make changes in their life. Not everyone figures out how to do that, and they waste extraordinary amounts of energy making half-hearted attempts and going about it the wrong way.

5. Identifying Your Non-Negotiables

Figure out what you really can't live without, then start simplifying the rest. Identify what you truly desire, not just what you _think_ you want. Focusing in on achieving those non-negotiables and leaving the rest alone will get you there faster.

6. Minimum Viable Products (MVP):

Test the market with the simplest version of your idea you can actually implement, then iterate based on the feedback and results you get. You'll save money and time on the front end, and you'll end up with a product that the market has demonstrated a need for. Apply the same mode of thinking to other areas of your life. If you want to stick to a new workout routine, keep it simple first and add layers as you go. For creatives, push out a complete draft of your work, then edit if necessary—don't self-edit for years to the exclusion of getting anything done.

7. Radical Candor:

Care Personally, Criticize Directly. Don't bullshit people, and care for them sincerely. Be constantly giving and soliciting meaningful feedback, and make sure you're giving positive feedback as often (if not more) than negative. Positive feedback communicates what you value, and you'll get more of it back.

8. Relentless Self-Reflection:

Give yourself feedback, too. Take some time out to record your goals and review your progress towards them. Be honest with yourself when you're not performing as well as you'd like, and feel glad when you are. Devoting some time to more introverted pursuits will help you know your truest self more fully, and that's a powerful tool for getting where you want to go.

A One-Week Challenge

I sincerely hope that by the time you've reached this point in the book, you're already trying out some changes to your routine that I've suggested in previous chapters. But if you haven't, or if you've only dipped your toe in, I'd challenge you to give it a sincere effort for just one week. For one week, go through and actually do the "Attack" exercises—one a day. In addition, try hansei sessions, journaling, meditation, or preferably all three for a few minutes each day. You have nothing to lose. If after a solid week you're convinced you're getting nothing out of it, fair enough—I'm glad you've still enjoyed the book enough to read it all, and I hope you come up with your own daily practices that help you stay focused. If you can't seem to make it a solid week, try again on another week. An inability to commit to something so small for a week without failing is its own impediment that will hinder you in other pursuits, so this is a good excuse to get over that.

Where to Go From Here

As the title says, go forth and conquer. I've tried to give you tools: practical techniques to use to focus yourself, as well as ways of thinking about life's complex challenges. You're ready to carry that forward and apply it to your own life. You may have already started. I hope you have. Just remember to take action and start implementing winning habits. Don't be a part of the 95% that are afraid to take the first step. Bit by bit, you'll see remarkable changes. When you do, I hope you'll share them.

Find like-minded individuals on the Internet or in person and try to hold each other accountable. Connect on social media and trade progress reports, talk through roadblocks, etc. If you form a community around *Breathe, Focus, Attack*, you'll make valuable connections with people who think about success in the same terms you do, which just may become your new secret weapon.

• • •

Most of all, I hope you keep in mind that change is possible. This whole book is about facilitating change. No matter where you're at now—even if you're going through the worst period of your life—you can put one foot in front of the other and get yourself to where you want to be. It might take a while, and it might be difficult, but it's possible. Your life is what you make of it, and when a challenge appears before you, you only need to do three things: take a breath, focus on the problem, and then attack.

About the Author

Ian Schechter is a serial entrepreneur. He also works with major brands on their marketing and Amazon strategies. He has his MBA from Binghamton University and is a prolific world traveler. You can follow him on Instagram: @ianadventures. He currently resides in New York City.

Made in the USA
San Bernardino, CA
05 July 2020